LIFESPICE
SALT-FREE
COOKBOOK

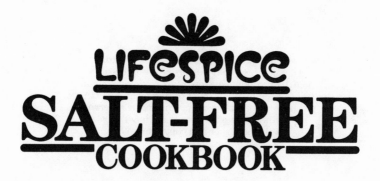

LIFESPICE
SALT-FREE
COOKBOOK

Ruth Baum and Hilary Baum

Illustrations by Nichole Keith

A PERIGEE BOOK

Perigee Books
are published by
The Putnam Publishing Group
200 Madison Avenue
New York, New York 10016

Published simultaneously in Canada by
General Publishing Co. Limited, Toronto

Library of Congress Cataloging in Publication Data

Baum, Ruth.
Lifespice salt free cookbook.

Includes index.
1. Salt-free diet—Recipes. I. Title
RM237.8.B38   1984   641.5'632   84-27393
SBN 0-399-51093-1

This book was designed and produced by
Footnote Productions Ltd.
6 Blundell Street
London N7 9BH

Composition by Point Blank
Printed by BookCrafters

Editorial Director: Sheila Rosenzweig
Art Director: Jon Dogar Marinesco
Illustrations: Nichole Keith

First Perigee Printing, 1985
Printed in the United States of America
1 2 3 4 5 6 7 8 9 10

*To our wonderful families
and to our dear Toto,
an always interested and eager taster.*

Acknowledgments

Many friends have contributed to this book in many ways.
Testing, tasting, typing and research were done by all in the best of spirits.
We would like to thank Florence Aaron for getting the Lifespice project moving,
Sam Aaron for selecting the wines for the menus, Ann Rowan for her large
contribution to the bread and dessert recipes, and Kate Phelan for her general
assistance and for sharing some of her grandmother's recipes with us.

The sodium and calorie counts were prepared by
Computrition in Chatsworth, California; we thank Bridget Harvey-Elliot, M.S., R.D.
for her help. We would also like to thank our editor, Glorya Hale, and
Sheila Rosenzweig and Tony Meisel for putting the book together.

We are grateful to our stellar cast of guest recipe contributors.
They all responded with gracious professionalism. Our very special thanks go to
James Beard, Craig Claiborne, Marion Cunningham, Pierre Franey, Barbara Kafka,
Felipe Rojas-Lombardi, Michael Tong, and Alfredo Viazzi.

Finally, we thank Uncle David Baum of Stanford University Medical School
for sharing his respected medical viewpoint on sodium in the diet.

Contents

Introduction

It all began in 1980 when we tasted some commercially prepared salt-free products, which we were told were the best then available. That taste experience could be summed up in one word: boring.

We were aware of the importance of limiting the amount of salt in the diet. Sodium overuse is associated with abnormally elevated blood pressure, or hypertension, a common health problem which can cause vascular disease in such critical organs as the heart, brain, and kidneys. By limiting sodium intake, the possibility of developing high blood pressure may be decreased. If the problem has already developed, limited sodium intake can help to control it.

We realized that there are three good ways to help prevent an excessive intake of salt. The first way is to increase consumption of foods naturally low in sodium, such as fresh fruits and vegetables, and to avoid food naturally high in sodium, such as shellfish and processed meats. The second is to read the labels of packaged foods carefully and to be wary of products which have salt listed among the first two or three ingredients; this usually indicates a generous amount of sodium. The third and most important way to reduce sodium intake is to learn to prepare dishes that are so attractive and flavorful that the absence of salt is not even noticed.

We are convinced that salt-free food can taste good, that by creatively using herbs, spices, and other ingredients, salt-free dishes can be interesting and delicious. And so we took up the challenge. Totally immersing ourselves in testing and tasting, we created a line of full-bodied condiments and salad dressings which are robust, satisfying — and salt-free. This is how the highly acclaimed Lifespice line of gourmet, salt-free condiments came into being.

In the course of developing the Lifespice condiments we also created salt-free recipes which proved what we had known all along — that cooking without salt is not synonymous with cooking without flavor. The wide selection of recipes in this book reflect this as well as our philosophy of cooking: we cook lightly and quickly; we use ingredients that are fresh, seasonal, and unprocessed; we balance flavors without the use of salt or chemical salt substitutes. In addition to being salt-free, our recipes are "light." We don't deep-fry, we use no heavy cream, very few eggs, and just a little bit of sweet butter, olive oil, and sugar.

Salt-free dishes aren't medicine — they are just delicious, healthful and easy to prepare. Just like any other dishes, those that are salt-free should have distinctive flavor and definite texture. They must, however, be prepared with special sensitivity because a little more thought — or at least a little different thought — about ingredients and flavor is required. All the ingredients in these recipes are naturally low in sodium. Consequently, some ingredients, Parmesan cheese and shrimp, for example, are not used. Our goal is to show you how to cook dishes so good that you'll never miss salt-laden food. We want you to enjoy what you *are* getting with this approach to eating — an appreciation of the flavors of well prepared and artfully seasoned dishes — and not regret what you're missing.

In our experience, many people, including many very good cooks, find a new interest and challenge in cooking when they start to make salt-free dishes. A burst of creativity seems to be mysteriously unlocked when people put away their saltshakers and foresake processed foods. We hope this book will help unlock that creativity in you.

Ruth Baum
Hilary Baum

Sodium Note

Salt is a naturally occurring substance consisting of 40 percent
sodium and 50 percent chloride. It is found in all living things and
is vital for many normal body functions. However, most doctors
agree that the amount of added sodium in the average diet should
be reduced. A normal diet with no added salt will provide the 1,100
to 3,000 milligrams (mg) of sodium generally needed daily by most
people. But because sodium is found not just in salt but also in other
common food additives such as sodium nitrate and MSG (mono-
sodium glutamate), we often consume far more than we realize.
All the recipes in this book list the amount of sodium and the
number of calories per serving. To give some perspective to the
sodium counts, the chart below lists the sodium content of some
common foods.

Sodium Content of Some Common Foods

1 teaspoon salt	2,196 mg
1 tablespoon unsalted butter	1 mg
1 cup low-fat milk	122 mg
1 pound tomatoes	14 mg
1 celery stalk	50 mg
1 pound potatoes	18 mg
1 cup all-purpose flour	2 mg
4 oz. shelled shrimp	159 mg
4 oz. fillet of sole	88 mg
8 oz. baked chicken, light meat, skin and bones removed	150 mg
1 oz. Parmesan cheese	455 mg

Accents

The imaginative use of herbs, spices, and other flavorings is of great importance to salt-free cooking. It is often not sufficient simply to eliminate the salt from a recipe; it must be replaced with something else to enhance the flavor of the dish. A full repertoire of seasonings, artfully used, will add interest and variety to food, bringing out the subtleties of natural flavor — all without salt.

In this chapter you will be introduced to the many alternatives to salt as a seasoning. You'll discover new ways to enliven your salt-free cooking using herbs, spices, oils, vinegars, and other condiments, many of which you can make yourself. As the recipes in this book prove, these accents are not only effective substitutes for salt, but the flavor they impart is actually preferable.

Many cooks tend at first to overcompensate for the missing salt. Go lightly. It's always easier to add a little dash more than is to subtract. Let your taste and the taste of the people you feed be the final judge.

Herbs

Herbs add character and interest to many dishes. Some fresh herbs are readily available at reasonable prices throughout the year. To store fresh herbs, rinse them well, blot them dry on paper towels, and store them in closed plastic bags. Punch a few small holes in the bags to let any condensation escape. You can store many herbs, particularly those that come with their roots, by putting the stems into a glass of water and covering the leaves with a plastic bag.

Sprigs, tied together, of fresh rosemary, thyme, fennel, or sage make an excellent basting brush. Use a herbal brush to baste broiled and barbecued food—the flavor of the herb will permeate the food as it cooks.

When you cook over charcoal or wood, add some sprigs of dried herbs to the fire. They will impart an herbal aroma to the food.

Dried herbs are a reasonable substitute for most fresh herbs. In cooking, the general rule is that one part of dried herbs is the equivalent to two to three parts of fresh herbs. For example, if a recipe calls for three teaspoons of chopped fresh dill, you can substitute one teaspoon of dried dill. Of course, the amount should be adjusted to suit your taste.

The flavor of dried herbs is best brought out by lightly crushing the leaves in a mortar and pestle or by rubbing them between the palms of your hands just before adding them to the food. The flavor of dried herbs can also be enhanced by sautéeing them in a little butter or oil or by soaking them in vinegar, stock, or hot water before adding them to a dish.

Much of the flavor of dried herbs is lost when they are not fresh. Prepackaged herbs have lost a great deal of their intensity by the time you purchase them. It is best, therefore, to buy dried herbs in small amounts and replenish your supplies frequently. Store dried herbs in small, tightly sealed jars in a cool, dry dark place.

Basil. Delicious in any tomato dish, basil is also great with mozzarella cheese, eggs, potatoes, and zucchini. Fresh basil is a must for the classic pesto sauce. Fresh basil leaves can be stored in a small container, the leaves covered with olive oil. The scented oil that remains after the leaves have been used will add wonderful flavor to sauces and salad dressings. Fresh basil leaves can also be preserved with a little olive oil in a blender or food processor. Pour the mixture into a small container and freeze. To use it, simply spoon some out and add it to the recipe. Basil is a good flavoring for herbed vinegar (see page 15). It is excellent, fresh or dried, in combination with rosemary in tomato sauce.

Chervil. Use chervil with fresh tomatoes and with fish. It adds a subtle flavor to salads and to cream soups. Chervil can be stored in the freezer in small plastic bags, but is best preserved in herb butter (see page 16).

Chives. Mild members of the onion family, chives add flavor to salads and soups of all kinds. They are often used as a garnish. Freeze chives in small plastic bags.

Dill. Fresh dill has an affinity for cucumbers, carrots, beets, beans, new potatoes, and summer squash. It is also used in many fish dishes and salads, for pickling and for garnishing. Dill is also good in combination with lemon and shallots. Dried dill retains much of its flavor. It also freezes well in small plastic bags.

Mint. The most refreshing of herbs, mint is used in herbal teas, fruit salads, lamb dishes, and vegetable salads. Try it, too, with carrots, leeks, zucchini, potatoes, and fresh peas. Dried mint retains its flavor.

Parsley. Widely available all year round, flat-leaved Italian parsley has more flavor than curly parsley, which makes an excellent garnish. Chopped fresh parsley will enhance most savory dishes.

Tarragon. A featured accent in many French dishes, tarragon goes particulary well with mushrooms, potatoes, eggs, carrots, poultry, and fish. Try it, too, in combination with lemon, mustard or shallots—and to make an herb vinegar (see page 15). Fresh tarragon is only available in summer, but dried tarragon has excellent flavor.

Thyme. The strong flavor of thyme is often a delightful surprise in a stew or soup or with roast pork or lamb. Thyme can be frozen in small plastic bags; however, dried thyme does have good flavor.

Rosemary. This strongly flavored herb is excellent with lamb, chicken, or in an olive-oil marinade. It freezes well and has excellent flavor when dried. Use it sparingly.

Coriander. Also known as cilantro, ulantro, Chinese parsley, and Mexican parsley, coriander is a pungent herb frequently used in Chinese, Indian, and Mexican cooking. The leaves are best when used fresh. Ground coriander is made from the seeds of the plant, not from its leaves.

Spices

Unlike herbs, which are always best used fresh, most spices are dried. Black peppercorns, for example, are dried berries, cloves are the dried buds of the clove tree, cinnamon is a dried bark, nutmeg is a dried seed (the dried fibrous covering of which is mace), and turmeric is a dried root. Nevertheless, the flavor of spices will diminish as the volatile oils that give them their aromatic character evaporate. If possible, buy spices in small quantities and replenish your supplies often. Discard any spices that are more than a year old. Store spices in small, tightly sealed jars and keep them in a cool, dark place.

It is best to buy spices in their whole form and prepare them as you need them. Freshly grated nutmeg, for example, is much more flavorful than preground nutmeg. Such spices as cumin seed can be "roasted" in a dry skillet over medium heat. Shake the pan often and cook until the seeds are light brown (about 10 minutes). Then pulverize the seeds in a mortar and pestle or in a small electric grinder; the aroma is intoxicating and the taste delicious.

Peppercorns. Pepper is, perhaps, the best and simplest seasoning in salt-free cooking. Pepper comes in many forms. Black peppercorns are the dried fruit of *Piper nigrum,* a climbing shrub. White pepper is made from the seeds of the ripe berries of the same plant or from black peppercorns from which the dark outer layer is removed. White pepper is less pungent than black pepper. Green peppercorns are the ripe berries which are preserved in vinegar. They have a mild flavor and aroma. Different varieties of *Piper nigrum* grown in different parts of the world vary in flavor and pungency.

Never use the ground black pepper that comes in jars or little metal boxes; thus packaged, the oils that give pepper its flavor and bite are almost gone. Use whole peppercorns and grind them yourself in a peppermill as needed. The pepper taste will be much more intense. The best peppermill is one that turns smoothly and can be adjusted to grind different degrees of coarseness.

Herb and Spice Blends

Many of the prepackaged herb and spice blends have salt or sugar added as extenders. It is possible, however, to find high-quality blends such as chili powder or curry powder that do not contain extenders. Always read the labels carefully before buying these products.

Blends of imported herbs are often sold in attractive containers. Buy these only for their decorative value and make your own blends using fresh ingredients.

Herb Vinegar

MAKES 2 CUPS

SODIUM PER SERVING: LESS THAN 0.5 MG
CALORIES PER SERVING: 3

Herb vinegars add additional depth of flavor to salad dressings, marinades and pickles, are easy to make and are an excellent way to preserve fresh herbs from your garden. Some favorite herbs for vinegar are tarragon, basil, rosemary and thyme. Whole garlic cloves or coarsely chopped shallots are also good additions.

3 to 6 fresh herb sprigs
2 cups white wine vinegar

Thoroughly wash a 1-pint bottle in soap and very hot water.
Rinse and blot dry the herbs.
Stuff the herbs into the bottle and add the vinegar.
Seal the bottle tightly with a cork or nonmetal cap.
Let stand in a cool, dark place for 2 weeks, gently shaking the bottle occasionally.

After 2 weeks, remove and discard the herbs. Strain the vinegar through cheesecloth into another bottle. Add more sprigs of the same fresh herbs to the bottle.

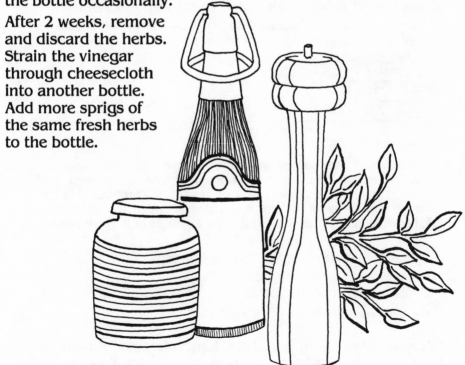

Herb Oil

MAKES 2 CUPS

SODIUM PER SERVING: LESS THAN 0.5 MG
CALORIES PER SERVING: 120

Herb oils, like herb vinegars, add flavor, especially to meat marinades. Strongly flavored herbs, such as basil, bay leaves, oregano, rosemary and thyme are recommended. Use them singly or in combination (with or without the addition of whole garlic cloves), and always use the best olive oil available.

7 to 10 fresh herb sprigs
2 cups high-quality olive oil

Thoroughly wash a 1-pint bottle in soap and very hot water.
Rinse and blot dry the herbs.
Stuff the herbs into the bottle.
Heat the olive oil in a small saucepan until it is hot but not boiling. Pour it into the bottle and seal tightly with a cork or other nonmetal cap. Let stand for 2 weeks. Then strain the oil through cheesecloth into another bottle. Discard the herbs. Add more sprigs of the same fresh herbs to the bottle.

Herb Butter

MAKES ¼ CUP

SODIUM PER SERVING (1 teaspoon): LESS THAN 0.5 MG
CALORIES PER SERVING: 26

A dab of herb butter spread on meat, fish, poultry, or vegetables, or mixed into rice or pasta, adds the aroma and flavor of the herb used. Try using parsley, tarragon, chervil, or basil. A tiny amount of finely chopped garlic, shallots or ginger can also be added. Instead of lemon juice or wine vinegar, try using other citrus juices or herb vinegars.

4 tablespoons unsalted butter, softened
3 tablespoons chopped fresh herbs
  or 2 teaspoons dried herbs
2 teaspoons lemon juice or vinegar

Combine the butter, herbs and lemon juice or vinegar in the container of a food processor or blender. Process until well blended. To make by hand, combine the ingredients in a small bowl and mix with a wooden spoon until well blended. Use immediately or freeze for later use.

Mushrooms

Fresh and dried mushrooms are useful for adding depth of flavor to salt-free dishes. Fresh cultivated mushrooms are readily available in any supermarket at a reasonable price. Woodland mushrooms such as cepes, morels, chanterelles and Japanese shiitaki are harder to find and rather more expensive. But they are worth the search and the price — and a small amount can go a long way.

Dried mushrooms are generally imported from the Orient or from Italy. They must be soaked before using (see pages 148 and 157). The soaking liquid can be strained and then used to add flavor to stocks and other cooking liquids.

Duxelles

MAKES 8 OUNCES

SODIUM PER SERVING (1 tablespoon): LESS THAN 0.5 MG
CALORIES PER SERVING: 5

Fresh mushrooms can be cooked down into a handy seasoning called duxelles. A spoonful of duxelles added to omelettes, gravies, sauces, or pasta or grain dishes adds a delicious mushroom flavor.

2 pounds fresh mushrooms
¼ pound unsalted butter
freshly ground black pepper

Rinse the mushrooms and wipe them dry with paper towels. Trim the ends of the stems if they are tough.

Finely chop the mushrooms with a large knife. Do not do this in a blender or food processor — the mushrooms will become too wet.

Melt the butter in a large, heavy skillet. Add the mushrooms and cook over low heat, uncovered, until almost all the liquid is gone and the mushrooms have turned dark, about 30 minutes. Stir occasionally. Add more butter if the mushrooms seem too dry. Season with black pepper to taste.

Put the duxelles into a tightly covered container and store in the refrigerator or freezer. To use frozen duxelles, simply cut off a piece with a knife and return the rest to the freezer. Add the unthawed duxelles to the other ingredients as they cook.

Mayonnaise

There are two inviolable rules for successfully making mayonnaise: the egg must be at room temperature and the oil must be added very, very slowly. Beyond that, feel free to experiment with the ingredients. Try different kinds of oil and vinegar, or try adding different seasonings.

Using the basic mayonnaise recipe below, a number of flavored mayonnaises can be made. To make garlic mayonnaise, add 1 to 2 crushed cloves of garlic for each egg yolk. For a tasty and colorful mayonnaise, add 1/8 teaspoon of crushed thyme and 1 tablespoon of finely diced tomato pulp or sweet red pepper.

Herb mayonnaise can be made when fresh herbs are available. For each egg yolk add 2 tablespoons of minced tarragon, basil, parsley, chives or watercress. Use a matching herb vinegar for additional flavor.

Mayonnaise Made by Hand

MAKES 1 CUP

SODIUM PER SERVING (1 tablespoon): 1 MG
CALORIES PER SERVING: 94

1 egg yolk, at room temperature
1 teaspoon vinegar or fresh lemon juice
1 to 2 teaspoons salt-free Dijon-style mustard or
    ½ teaspoon dry mustard
¾ cup oil
freshly ground black pepper to taste

Combine the egg yolk, vinegar, mustard, and pepper in a small mixing bowl. With a wire whisk or heavy fork, beat until the mixture starts to thicken.

Add the oil *very* slowly, starting a drop at a time and then in a slow, steady stream, beating until it is completely incorporated. If the mayonnaise is too thick, add more vinegar or lemon juice to thin.

Mayonnaise Made in the Blender

MAKES 1 CUP

SODIUM PER SERVING (1 tablespoon): 1 MG
CALORIES PER SERVING: 98

1 whole egg, at room temperature
1 teaspoon vinegar or fresh lemon juice
1 to 2 teaspoons salt-free Dijon-style mustard
 or ½ teaspoon dry mustard
¾ cup oil
freshly ground black pepper to taste

Put the egg, vinegar, mustard, and pepper in the container of a blender or food processsor. Blend at low speed until the mixture starts to thicken.

Add the oil *very* slowly, starting a drop at a time and then in a slow, steady stream, blending until it is completely incorporated. If the mayonnaise is too thick, add more vinegar or lemon juice to thin.

Tartar Sauce

MAKES 1½ CUPS

SODIUM PER SERVING (1 tablespoon): 3 MG
CALORIES PER SERVING: 68

Tartar sauce is basically a mayonnaise with added texture. Besides serving it with fish, try it with cold chicken instead of plain mayonnaise.

1 cup Mayonnaise (see above)
2 tablespoons chopped sweet salt-free pickles
 or Overnight Cucumber Pickles (see page 31)
1 tablespoon chopped parsley or dill
1 chopped hard-cooked egg
 or chopped white of 1 hard-cooked egg
1 tablespoon wine vinegar

In a small bowl, gently mix the mayonnaise, pickles, parsley or dill, egg and vinegar together.

Vinaigrette

MAKES ABOUT ¾ CUP

SODIUM PER SERVING (1 teaspoon): LESS THAN 0.5 MG
CALORIES PER SERVING: 30

One of the most important — and easiest — accents is vinaigrette.
It has dozens of uses in addition to being an excellent salad dressing.
If you like a lot of garlic, use a minced garlic clove. If you prefer just a
hint of garlic, use a whole clove. And if you prefer no garlic at all, leave
it out. Generally, the ratio of oil to vinegar in vinaigrette is three to one,
but you can vary the proportions to your taste. Vinaigrette will keep for
weeks in the refrigerator. Let it warm up to room temperature and mix
well before using.

1 minced or *whole garlic clove (optional)*
freshly ground black pepper
⅛ teaspoon dry mustard
    or ¼ teaspoon salt-free prepared mustard
3 to 4 tablespoons wine vinegar or *lemon juice*
9 tablespoons olive oil

If using minced garlic, put it in a small bowl along with
black pepper to taste and the mustard. Mash the garlic into
the pepper and mustard with the back of a spoon. Add the
vinegar. With a fork or small whisk, beat in the oil, a little
at a time. If using a whole
garlic clove, add it at this
point. Let dressing sit for
15 minutes. Whisk before
serving and discard
the garlic clove.

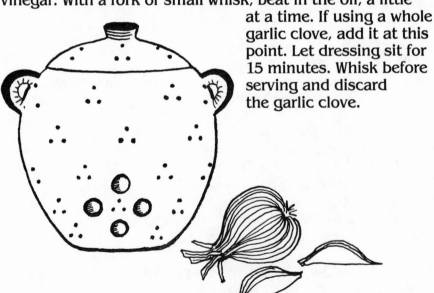

Tomato Dressing

MAKES ¾ CUP

SODIUM PER SERVING (1 tablespoon): 4 MG
CALORIES PER SERVING: 3

This oil-free, low-calorie dressing is excellent on simple green salads.

½ cup salt-free tomato juice
1 tablespoon red wine vinegar
1 tablespoon finely minced sweet onion
2 tablespoons chopped fresh dill
½ teaspoon finely chopped garlic (optional)
¼ teaspoon dry mustard

Put all the ingredients into a small jar with a tightly fitting lid. Seal the jar and shake well to mix the ingredients. Refrigerate for 1 hour to allow the dressing to thicken.

Basic Yogurt Dressing

MAKES ¾ CUP

SODIUM PER SERVING (1 tablespoon): 7 MG
CALORIES PER SERVING: 8

The tangy flavor of the yogurt in this oil-free dressing complements any salad. Almost any combination of two or three herbs, such as thyme, tarragon, chervil, dill, mint, parsley and basil, will give the dressing character.

½ cup unflavored low-fat yogurt
1 tablespoon plus 1 teaspoon red wine vinegar
1 garlic clove, minced (optional)
1 teaspoon crushed dried tarragon
2 tablespoons chopped fresh parsley
freshly ground black pepper
1 teaspoon salt-free Dijon-style mustard

Put the yogurt into a small bowl. Add the vinegar, garlic, tarragon, parsley, black pepper to taste and the mustard. Mix well and pour over salad.

Basic Marinade

MAKES 1 CUP

SODIUM PER RECIPE: 6 MG
CALORIES PER RECIPE: 1,035

A marinade adds flavor and juiciness to food that will later be barbecued or broiled. If the marinating time is two hours or less, the food can be kept at room temperature. When marinating for longer than two hours the food must be refrigerated. Always turn the food often while it is marinating. Use leftover marinade to baste the food as it cooks. The basic marinade recipe given here calls for oregano but almost any dried herb or combination of herbs, such as thyme, rosemary, tarragon and dill, may be used.

½ cup olive oil
¼ cup red wine
¼ cup red wine vinegar or *lemon juice*
3 garlic cloves, crushed
1 teaspoon dried oregano
freshly ground black pepper

Combine all the ingredients in a glass or ceramic dish large enough to hold the food being marinated. Mix well.

Add the food and turn it to coat well.
Marinate food as directed.

Quick Poaching Stock

MAKES 2 CUPS

SODIUM PER RECIPE: 9 MG
CALORIES PER RECIPE: 65

This delicious stock can be made quickly. Use it for poaching chicken or fish. For a larger amount of stock, simply double the recipe. To poach a large whole fish, double the recipe and prepare it in a large, shallow skillet. Leftover stock can be kept in the refrigerator for a few days. It freezes well.

2 cups water
¼ cup dry vermouth or *white wine*
2 garlic cloves
3 parsley or dill sprigs
freshly ground black pepper

Put the water, vermouth, garlic, parsley or dill and black pepper to taste into a small saucepan. Simmer gently for 10 minutes.

Add the ingredient to be poached. Cover the saucepan and simmer over low heat until done.

Tomato Condiment

MAKES 12 OUNCES

SODIUM PER SERVING (1 tablespoon): 3 MG
CALORIES PER SERVING: 16

A spoonful or two of tomato condiment adds depth of flavor to any cooking sauce, stew, or vegetable dish. It's also a good all-purpose tomato sauce or ketchup. Try it on broiled fish. It will keep well in the refrigerator for about three weeks.

3 tablespoons grated and well-drained fresh horseradish
1 green pepper, seeded and quartered
2 medium onions, quartered
½ cup water
1 14-ounce can salt-free tomato purée
1 teaspoon dry mustard
1 tablespoon sugar
1½ tablespoons cider vinegar
½ teaspoon ground cloves
1 teaspoon hot red pepper flakes
1 bay leaf

In a food processor, blender or by hand, chop the horseradish, green pepper and onions as finely as possible. Put into a medium-sized saucepan and add the water, tomato purée, mustard, sugar, vinegar, ground cloves, red pepper flakes and bay leaf. Mix well. Cover the saucepan and simmer over low heat for 20 minutes. Remove the bay leaf.

Serve hot as a sauce or cold as a condiment.

Hot Mustard

MAKES ½ CUP

SODIUM PER SERVING (1 tablespoon): LESS THAN 0.5 MG
CALORIES PER SERVING: 39

This is the simplest way to make a quick and hot mustard. Be sure to let it stand for at least 20 minutes — otherwise it will be bitter. To make a mustard relish, add 1 teaspoon of honey (or more or less to taste) and ¼ cup of chopped Overnight Cucumber Pickles (see page 31).

6 tablespoons dry mustard, preferably Coleman's
5 tablespoons water

Put the dry mustard into a small bowl.
Gradually add the liquid and stir until all lumps are dissolved.
Set aside for at least 20 minutes before serving.

Coarse Sweet Mustard

MAKES 1 CUP

SODIUM PER SERVING (1 tablespoon): LESS THAN 0.5 MG
CALORIES PER SERVING: 20

Homemade mustard is a wonderful accent to have on hand.
Covered tightly after each use, it will keep in the refrigerator for several months. Use it whenever a recipe calls for mustard. Put some into a decorative jar and you have a delightful gift.

¼ cup white or brown mustard seeds
⅓ cup cider vinegar
¼ cup white wine
¼ cup water
2 teaspoons honey
¼ teaspoon ground allspice
⅛ teaspoon ground turmeric

Put the mustard seeds, vinegar, and wine into a small bowl. Set aside for 3 hours.

Put the mustard seed mixture, water, honey, allspice and turmeric into the bowl of a food processor. Using the steel blade, process into a coarse purée, about 2 minutes.

Pour the mixture into the top of a double boiler. Cook over simmering water for 10 minutes, stirring occasionally. Pour into a bowl to cool.

When the mustard is cool, scrape it into a jar with a tightly fitting lid. Keep refrigerated.

Ginger

Fresh ginger root is an important flavoring ingredient for the salt-free kitchen. It is particularly good for adding zest to stir-fried dishes, stews, soups and marinades. Dried ground ginger is no substitute for the real thing, much of which is now grown in Hawaii. Fresh ginger root is available throughout the year in most supermarkets and specialty food stores. To store fresh ginger, wrap it tightly in plastic wrap and keep it in the vegetable drawer of the refrigerator. Alternatively, cut the root into smaller pieces, peel them, put them into a jar, add enough sherry to cover and store in the refrigerator — or pickle the ginger, using the recipe below. Ginger in sherry or pickled ginger can be substituted in any recipe that calls for fresh ginger.

Pickled Ginger

MAKES 1 PINT

SODIUM PER SERVING (1 teaspoon): LESS THAN 0.5 MG
CALORIES PER SERVING: 3

In Japan, pickled ginger is always served with sushi and sashimi. It's also a wonderful condiment to serve with fish or meat. And it adds real zing to chicken salad. Pickled, it will keep indefinitely if it is submerged in the pickling liquid.

2 tablespoons sugar
1 cup rice wine vinegar
½ cup water
½ pound fresh ginger root

Combine the sugar, vinegar, and water in a 1-pint jar that has a tight lid.

Peel the ginger and cut it into long, paper-thin slices using a swivel-bladed vegetable peeler. Submerge the pieces of ginger in the pickling liquid. Refrigerate for 2 or 3 weeks before using.

Confetti Corn Relish

MAKES 3½ CUPS
_____

SODIUM PER SERVING (1 tablespoon): LESS THAN 0.5 MG
CALORIES PER SERVING: 18

Crunchy and colorful, this relish is a great side dish to serve with sandwiches. It will keep for two weeks when stored in the refrigerator in a tightly covered jar.

3 cups cooked corn, scraped from the cob
½ sweet red pepper, seeded and diced
½ green pepper, seeded and diced
4 whole scallions, thinly sliced
½ teaspoon ground cumin
3 tablespoons vegetable oil
1½ tablespoons wine vinegar
freshly ground black pepper to taste

Put the corn into a serving bowl. Add the remaining ingredients and mix well.

Paula's Quick Onion Relish

MAKES 1 CUP
_____

SODIUM PER SERVING (1 tablespoon): 1 MG
CALORIES PER SERVING: 4

Paula Peck was a wonderful cook and a dear friend. Her skills in the kitchen were dazzling. She often served this simple relish, which is delicious made fresh and served with broiled meat and curry dishes. It will keep well in the refrigerator for several days.

1 medium-sized sweet onion, coarsely chopped
fresh lemon juice
¼ teaspoon red pepper flakes

Put the chopped onions into a small bowl and add lemon juice to cover. Add the red pepper flakes and mix well. Cover the bowl tightly and refrigerate until ready to use.

Garden Relish

MAKES APPROXIMATELY 2½ QUARTS

SODIUM PER SERVING (1 tablespoon): 2 MG
CALORIES PER SERVING: 7

This relish can be made year round. For the red peppers you can
substitute additional green pepper and carrot.

5 cups shredded cabbage
4 cups diced onion
2 cups diced green pepper
2 cups diced red pepper
1½ cups diced carrot
1 tablespoon celery seeds
1 tablespoon mustard seeds
1½ cups white wine vinegar
¼ cup water
½ cup sugar

Remove as much liquid as possible from the vegetables
by wringing them in a clean kitchen towel or by putting
them into a colander and pressing with a heavy weight for
about 1 hour.

Put the vegetables into a large bowl.

Tie the celery and mustard seeds into a square of cheesecloth or put them into a tea egg.

Put the vinegar, water, sugar and celery and mustard
seeds into an enameled saucepan. Bring to a boil and
cook for 5 minutes. Remove the celery and mustard seeds,
discard half, and put the remaining half loose into the liquid.

Pour the liquid over the vegetables. Mix well.

Sterilize 5 1-pint jars by washing them with soap and
very hot water and then placing them, upside-down, in 4
to 5 inches of boiling water. Boil the jars over low heat for
8 minutes. Turn off the heat and add the lids and rings to
the hot water. Let stand for 3 minutes.

Divide the relish mixture evenly among the jars while the
jars are still hot. Fill the jars to within ½ inch of the top,
making sure that there is enough liquid to cover the relish

in each jar. Run a knife down along the insides of the jars
to release any air bubbles. Seal the jars tightly with the hot
lids. Cool the jars in a draft-free place overnight. The next
day, check the seals by turning the jars upside down or
pressing the center of the inner lids. If there is no leakage
or if the inner lids do not move, then the jars are sealed
properly. Store the jars in the refrigerator. The relish can be
served at once.

Megan's Cranberry Velvet Conserve

MAKES 2½ CUPS

SODIUM PER SERVING (1 tablespoon): LESS THAN 0.5 MG
CALORIES PER SERVING: 31

This rich cranberry conserve is the invention of Megan More, a chef and
caterer in New York and Palm Beach. Serve it with turkey or any other
poultry or broiled meat.

½ cup walnut halves
3 navel oranges, peeled and sectioned
1 12-ounce package fresh cranberries
½ cup water
½ cup orange juice
3 tablespoons sugar
2 tablespoons salt-free tomato paste
1 6-ounce package frozen raspberries
3 tablespoons brandy

Put the walnut halves and the orange sections into the
bowl of a food processor or blender and process until finely
chopped, or chop by hand with a heavy knife. Set aside.

Sort and rinse the cranberries.

In a large saucepan, combine the water, orange juice,
and sugar. Bring to a boil. Add the cranberries and return
to a boil. Reduce the heat and simmer for 5 minutes,
stirring occasionally.

Stir in the tomato paste, raspberries, and brandy and cook
for 5 minutes more or until the raspberries just thaw.

Pour the cranberry mixture into a serving bowl.
Add the walnut and orange mixture and toss gently.
Serve at room temperature.

Pesto Sauce with Walnuts

MAKES APPROXIMATELY 3 CUPS

SODIUM PER SERVING (1 tablespoon): 1 MG
CALORIES PER SERVING: 71

Pesto is a delightful Italian sauce for just about anything — including
pasta, fish, chicken and vegetables. Try adding a spoonful to a bowl of
plain chicken soup. We use walnuts in pesto because they are the lowest
in sodium of any nuts, but pine nuts *(pignoli)*, which are traditional in
pesto, may be used instead. Pesto will keep in the refrigerator for at least
a week and freezes well. If you are planning to freeze it, omit the nuts.
Fresh basil is available most of the year in many supermarkets. Basil
leaves layered in oil and stored in the refrigerator in a tightly closed jar
will keep well for several weeks. When fresh basil is not available,
3 cups of parsley and 1 tablespoon dried basil can be substituted.
Do not attempt to make pesto using dried basil alone!

3 cups tightly packed fresh basil leaves
1 cup chopped walnuts
3 garlic cloves, minced
2 tablespoons grated low-sodium hard cheese (optional)
1 cup olive oil
freshly ground black pepper

In a food processor or blender or by hand, chop the basil
leaves finely.

Mix the chopped basil with the walnuts, garlic and cheese,
either in a food processor or blender or by hand. Add the oil
in a thin, steady stream, blending it well with the other
ingredients. Add black pepper to taste.

Barbecue Sauce

MAKES 1 PINT

SODIUM PER SERVING (¼ cup): 15 MG
CALORIES PER SERVING: 48

This spicy barbecue sauce can be used in all the traditional ways as well as for a topping for baked potatoes, as an ingredient in Meatless Chili (see page 152), or as a sauce for tacos.

6 ounces salt-free tomato paste
¾ cup water
¾ cup cider vinegar
1 tablespoon plus 1 teaspoon chili powder
1 teaspoon minced garlic
¼ teaspoon cayenne pepper
½ teaspoon ground cumin
1 tablespoon safflower oil
2 tablespoons honey

Put the tomato paste and water into a medium-sized saucepan. Stir well and simmer over medium heat for 2 minutes.

Add the vinegar, chili powder, garlic, cayenne pepper, cumin, safflower oil, and honey. Mix well. Simmer for 15 minutes, stirring frequently.

Dilly Beans

MAKES 1 PINT

SODIUM PER RECIPE: 22 MG
CALORIES PER RECIPE: 108

These pickled green beans remain crisp and crunchy for days. The recipe can easily be doubled or tripled.

½ pound fresh green beans, trimmed
6 fresh dill sprigs, thick stems removed
2 garlic cloves
¼ teaspoon cayenne pepper
1 teaspoon dill seeds
¾ cup distilled white vinegar
¾ cup boiling water

Thoroughly wash a 1-pint Mason jar in soap and hot water.

Cook the green beans in a large pot of rapidly boiling water for 2 minutes. Drain well and rinse under cold running water to set the color.

Put 3 dill sprigs into the bottom of the jar. Add the garlic cloves, cayenne pepper and dill seeds. Tightly pack the jar with the green beans. Top with the remaining dill sprigs. Fill the jar halfway with the vinegar, then fill to within ½ inch of the top with the boiling water.

Tightly seal the jar. Let cool and then refrigerate. Let the green beans pickle at least overnight. Serve chilled.

Overnight Cucumber Pickles

MAKES 1½ QUARTS

SODIUM PER RECIPE: 54 MG
CALORIES PER RECIPE: 142

These easy-to-make pickles should be stored in tightly covered glass jars in the refrigerator, where they will stay crisp for at least a week. They are a refreshing accompaniment to sandwiches and cold meats, and they're also delicious as a low-calorie snack just by themselves. You can make them with zucchini spears instead of cucumbers.

5 medium-sized cucumbers, about 1 pound
  (Kirby cucumbers are preferable)
2 garlic cloves, crushed
2 dried red chili peppers
  or ¼ teaspoon hot red pepper flakes
5 allspice berries
2 bay leaves
10 black peppercorns
6 to 8 fresh dill sprigs
1 cup distilled vinegar
1 cup water

Peel, quarter, and seed the cucumbers.

Put all the ingredients into a large bowl or into jars. Cover tightly. Refrigerate overnight before eating.

Apple Ginger Chutney

MAKES 6 PINTS

SODIUM PER SERVING (1 tablespoon): 2 MG
CALORIES PER SERVING: 22

Chutney is a good accompaniment to simple dishes. The fruit and
spices add zest to broiled meat and poultry, steamed vegetables, and
mild cheeses. Try chutney on a sandwich instead of mustard or ketchup.
Chutney also makes a good gift from your kitchen.

3 cups cider vinegar
4 cups brown sugar
*10 cups (4 to 5 pounds) peeled, cored, and diced
    firm, tart apples*
4 lemons with rinds, chopped and seeded
2 medium-sized onions, chopped
5 large garlic cloves, chopped
½ cup peeled and finely chopped fresh ginger
1½ cups dark raisins
1 teaspoon cayenne pepper

In a large saucepan over low heat, bring the cider vinegar
and sugar to a simmer. Add the diced apples and cook until
the mixture returns to a simmer. Add the remaining ingredients and cook gently for 20 minutes, stirring occasionally.

Spoon the chutney into clean glass jars and seal tightly.
Store the jars in the refrigerator. The chutney will keep well
for 4 to 6 weeks.

Beginnings

Appetizers, hôrs d'oeuvres, canapés and antipasti are basically different terms for the same thing — food, often accompanied by drinks, served as the start to a meal. We call these predining delicacies simply beginnings.

The goal of a beginning is to arouse interest and desire for the meal to follow — to whet the appetite. To this end, the taste, color, and texture of this introductory course should complement and contrast with the main course. If, for example, the main course is Broiled Fish Fillets with Green Sauce (see page 83), which has a soft texture, serve something crunchy, such as Spiced Nuts (see page 36) or Salsa (see page 41) with raw vegetables, as the beginning.

Because a beginning is the prelude to the main course, servings are generally small. The appetite must be stimulated, not sated. Many of the recipes given here, however, could also be served in larger quantities as a main dish. Many can also be made ahead and kept on hand for unexpected guests or unexpected appetites.

Salty foods are often served as beginnings. Olives, anchovies, cheese, salted and smoked meats and fish, salted nuts and pretzels are traditional, largely because they are thought to go well with drinks. Actually, the saltiness of these foods (not to mention the preservatives and other artificial ingredients in them) actually dulls the palate, making the meal to follow less enjoyable.

The recipes in this chapter use a variety of spices and ingredients instead of salt to make interesting, delicious and healthful beginnings that are the start to truly good meals.

Nachos

SERVES 4 TO 6

SODIUM PER SERVING: 6 MG
CALORIES PER SERVING: 188

If you like your nachos really hot, sprinkle some chopped green chili pepper over the cheese before baking. Serve with Salsa (see page 41).

8 ounces salt-free tortilla chips
½ cup grated low-sodium Monterey Jack cheese
Salsa (see page 41)

Preheat the oven to 400°F.

Put the tortilla chips on an ovenproof platter or baking sheet. Sprinkle the cheese evenly over the chips. Spread the salsa over the cheese, using about ½ teaspoon per chip.

Bake until the cheese is melted and bubbly, about 4 minutes. Serve warm.

Grilled Kebabs

SERVES 4

SODIUM PER SERVING: 43 MG
CALORIES PER SERVING: 116

Kebabs can be made from many combinations. It is important, however, to cut all the ingredients to the same size and to combine those that have the same cooking time. Chicken livers or cubed lamb are good meats for kebabs; thick fish steaks such as swordfish, salmon, and halibut are also delicious when grilled. Because they retain less heat, bamboo skewers are preferable to metal.

1 whole chicken breast, skinned, boned and cubed
1 medium-sized zucchini, cubed
½ pound small white pearl onions
1 pint cherry tomatoes

Marinade:

¼ cup olive oil
⅓ cup wine vinegar
1 garlic clove, minced
6 peppercorns
*1 teaspoon dried or 1 tablespoon chopped fresh rosemary,
    sage, and/or thyme*
juice of ½ lemon or lime

Combine the ingredients for the marinade in a large bowl.

Add the chicken and vegetables to the marinade. Toss to coat the ingredients with the marinade. Refrigerate for at least 2 hours, turning frequently.

Remove the chicken and vegetables from the marinade with a slotted spoon. Drain on paper towels.

Thread the chicken and vegetables pieces alternately on skewers, beginning and ending each kebab with a pearl onion.

Place the kebabs in a shallow baking pan under a preheated broiler or on a grill over hot coals. To grill, cook, turning frequently and basting with the marinade, for about 10 minutes, or until the vegetables are slightly charred outside and soft inside, and the chicken is thoroughly cooked.
To broil, follow the same cooking procedure, but cook for 15 minutes.

Eggplant Salad

SERVES 6

SODIUM PER SERVING: 7 MG
CALORIES PER SERVING: 65

Serve this tasty salad as a first course on individual plates garnished with cherry tomatoes or as a spread or dip with raw vegetables, crackers, or thinly sliced bread.

2 medium eggplants
2 ripe tomatoes, seeded and chopped
4 whole scallions, finely chopped
freshly ground black pepper
1 tablespoon olive oil
1 tablespoon lemon juice
½ cup chopped fresh parsley

Preheat the oven to 450°F.

Put the eggplants on a baking sheet. Roast them, turning them frequently, for about 25 minutes, or until the skin is brown and the juices just start to run.

When the eggplants are cool enough to handle, peel them and cut them in quarters. Remove the seeds. Chop the eggplant finely.

Put the chopped eggplant, tomatoes, and scallions into a large bowl.

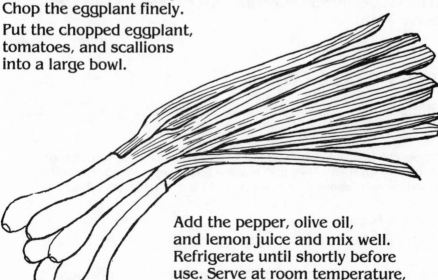

Add the pepper, olive oil, and lemon juice and mix well. Refrigerate until shortly before use. Serve at room temperature, garnished with chopped parsley.

Spiced Nuts

MAKES 2 CUPS

SODIUM PER SERVING (¼ cup): 7 MG
CALORIES PER SERVING: 249

These nuts, served warm or at room temperature, are particularly good with drinks. We make them with walnuts because they are low in sodium, but filberts, almonds, and pecans are also good. Instead of chili powder, try spicing the nuts with coarsely ground black pepper, cumin, oregano, or curry powder. Store the nuts in an airtight container, but do not refrigerate.

2 cups shelled walnuts
¼ cup melted sweet butter
1½ teaspoons chili powder

Preheat the oven to 350°F.

Melt the butter in a skillet.
Add the nuts and toss well to coat.

Arrange the nuts in one layer on a metal baking sheet.

Roast the nuts, turning them frequently for even cooking, for 25 minutes, or until they are lightly toasted.

With a slotted spoon, remove the nuts and put them in a serving dish. Sprinkle with the chili powder. Mix well. Serve warm.

Spicy Chicken Wings

SERVES 6

SODIUM PER SERVING: 70 MG
CALORIES PER SERVING: 213

These chicken wings are good as an hôrs d'oeuvre. Be sure to pass napkins with them. They also make a fine main course served with Noodles with Peanut Sauce (see page 128) and crisp green beans.

2 pounds chicken wings
1 cup Barbecue Sauce (see page 30)

Remove and discard the tips from the chicken wings, then cut the membrane between the joints. Put the chicken wings into a shallow baking dish large enough to hold them in one layer. Pour the barbecue sauce over the wings and turn each piece to coat well. Refrigerate for 3 to 4 hours before cooking, turning the wings occasionally.

Preheat the oven to 375ºF.

Bake the wings for about 30 minutes or until they are well glazed. Turn them occasionally and baste with the pan juices.

Michael Tong's Chicken Soong
(Cubed Chicken in Lettuce Leaves)

SERVES 4 TO 6

SODIUM PER SERVING: 99 MG
CALORIES PER SERVING: 186

Michael Tong is a wonderful chef with a vast knowledge of Chinese cuisine. He is the proprietor of two well-known Chinese restaurants in New York City, Shun Lee Palace and Shun Lee West. The chili paste with garlic used in this recipe is available in most Oriental markets.

1 head iceberg lettuce
1 large whole chicken breast, skinned and boned
1 egg white
2 long green chili peppers
½ cup drained canned water chestnuts
½ cup finely diced celery
3 teaspoons finely diced carrot
1 teaspoon finely chopped ginger root
2 teaspoons finely chopped garlic
3 teaspoons finely chopped scallion (white part only)
2 teaspoons dry sherry
½ teaspoon chili paste with garlic
2 tablespoons vegetable oil
½ teaspoon sesame oil

Core the lettuce and separate the head into leaves. Arrange the leaves on a serving platter and set aside.

Put the chicken breast onto a flat working surface. Holding

a sharp knife almost parallel to the working surface, cut the breast into the thinnest possible slices. Stack the slices and cut them into shreds. Cut the shreds into tiny cubes. There should be about 2 cups.

Put the chicken cubes into a mixing bowl. Add the egg white and mix well. Cover the bowl and refrigerate for at least 30 minutes.

Seed the chili peppers. Cut them in half lengthwise, then cut each half into very thin strips. Cut the strips into small cubes. There should be about ½ cup.

Slice the water chestnuts thinly. Stack the slices and cut them into small cubes. There should be about ½ cup.

In a small bowl, combine the chili peppers, water chestnuts, celery, carrot, and ginger. Mix well and set aside.

In another small bowl, combine the garlic and scallion. Mix well and set aside.

In another small bowl, combine the sherry and the chili paste with garlic. Mix well and set aside.

Heat the vegetable oil in a wok or heavy skillet. When the oil is very hot, add the chicken cubes. Sauté for 2 minutes, stirring constantly to separate the cubes. Remove the chicken from the wok or skillet with a slotted spoon. Put the cubes into a bowl and set aside.

Add the garlic and scallions, and more vegetable oil if necessary, to the wok or skillet. Sauté the garlic and scallions, stirring constantly, for 1 minute. Add the celery and water chestnut mixture and sauté, stirring constantly, for 30 seconds more. Add the sherry and chili paste mixture. Sauté, stirring constantly, for 30 seconds more.

Return the chicken cubes to the wok or skillet. Sauté, stirring constantly, until the chicken is very hot. Add the sesame oil and stir rapidly. Transfer the mixture to a heated serving platter.

Serve the chicken mixture with the lettuce on the side. Each diner should put a large spoonful of the chicken mixture on a lettuce leaf. Fold or roll the lettuce before eating.

Mushroom Pate in Tomato Shells

SERVES 6

SODIUM PER SERVING: 16 MG
CALORIES PER SERVING: 173

This delicious pâté may be used to fill tomato shells, as suggested here, or molded into a loaf and served with thin toast. A mixture of such mushrooms as shiitake and golden oak adds texture and flavor.

2 tablespoons unsalted butter
1 pound fresh mushrooms, coarsely chopped
6 shallots, diced
2 garlic cloves, minced
¼ cup chopped parsley
½ cup walnut halves
¼ teaspoon freshly ground black pepper
4 tablespoons Vinaigrette (see page 20)
3 firm, ripe tomatoes

Melt the butter in a heavy skillet over medium heat. Add the mushrooms, shallots, garlic, and parsley. Cook, stirring frequently, until the ingredients are soft and the mushrooms begin to give up their liquid.

Remove the mushroom mixture from the skillet with a slotted spoon, draining as much liquid from it as possible. Put the mixture into a bowl and set aside.

In a blender or food processor, or by hand using a heavy knife, finely chop all but six of the walnut halves.

Add the chopped walnuts to the mushroom mixture. Add the vinaigrette and the black pepper. Mix well.

Cut each tomato in half. Scoop out the pulp and seeds. (A grapefruit knife or a round spoon does the job well.) Turn the shells upside down to drain.

Fill each tomato shell with a mound of the mushroom pâté. Top each with a walnut half.

Seviche

SERVES 6

SODIUM PER SERVING: 46 MG
CALORIES PER SERVING: 184

Seviche, a South American dish, is a light and refreshing first course.
Serve it in small bowls or on a bed of lettuce leaves. The lime juice
"cooks" the raw fish. Use any firm-fleshed fish, such as halibut, scrod,
red snapper, or tilefish. Scallops (whole if using small bay scallops, halved
if using large sea scallops) are often used for this dish, but they are
high in sodium.

2 large, ripe tomatoes
1 pound very fresh fish fillets cut into 1-inch cubes
4 whole scallions, chopped
½ cucumber, peeled, seeded, and diced
1 small sweet red pepper, seeded and finely chopped
⅔ cup fresh lime juice
¼ cup olive oil
¼ teaspoon hot red pepper flakes
½ cup finely chopped fresh coriander
   or ½ cup finely chopped fresh parsley
   and 1 teaspoon dried coriander

Blanch the tomatoes by placing them in a large pot of boiling
water for about 10 seconds. Drain the tomatoes.
When they are cool enough to handle, peel them with a
small, sharp knife. Seed and chop the tomatoes.

Put the fish cubes into a large bowl. Add the scallions,
cucumbers, and tomatoes. Toss gently.

In a small bowl, combine the lime juice, olive oil, and red
pepper flakes. Mix well.

Add the lime juice mixture to the fish mixture.
Add the coriander. Mix gently.

Marinate the seviche in the refrigerator for 2 to 4 hours.
Mix gently before serving.

Salsa
(Mexican Hot Sauce)

MAKES 2½ CUPS

SODIUM PER SERVING (2 tablespoons): 2 MG
CALORIES PER SERVING: 16

This refreshing sauce can be served with cold meats or poultry, used as a taco dip, or as a delicious salad dressing for crisp greens. It is also good as a dip for the salt-free corn and potato chips now available in most supermarkets.

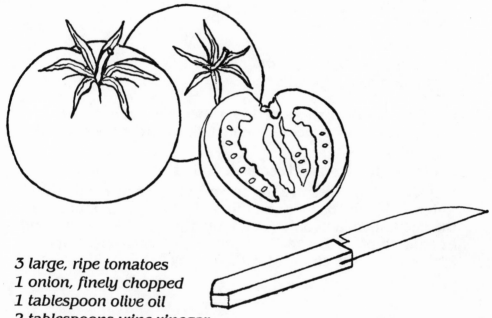

3 large, ripe tomatoes
1 onion, finely chopped
1 tablespoon olive oil
2 tablespoons wine vinegar
½ to ¾ long green chili pepper, seeded and finely chopped
2 tablespoons chopped fresh coriander or fresh parsley

Blanch the tomatoes by placing them in a large pot of boiling water for about 10 seconds. Drain the tomatoes. When they are cool enough to handle, peel with a small, sharp knife. Seed and chop the tomatoes.

Combine the tomatoes and onion in a large bowl. Add the oil and vinegar and mix well. Add green chili to taste, beginning with half the chili pepper.

Sprinkle with the fresh coriander or parsley.

Dilled Cucumber Salad

SERVES 6

SODIUM PER SERVING: 5 MG
CALORIES PER SERVING: 30

Serve this refreshing salad as a first course or as a side dish with fish, cold poultry or a sandwich.

2 large cucumbers, peeled and thinly sliced
3 whole scallions, thinly sliced
2 tablespoons sugar
2 tablespoons white vinegar
4 tablespoons water
¼ teaspoon coarsely ground black pepper
¼ cup chopped fresh dill

Put the cucumber slices between sheets of paper towel. With your hands, squeeze as much liquid from the cucumber slices as possible.

Put the cucumbers and scallions into a serving bowl.

In a small bowl, dissolve the sugar in the vinegar. Add the water and black pepper and mix well. Pour the mixture over the cucumbers and onions and mix well. Let the salad stand at room temperature for 10 minutes to blend the flavors. Sprinkle with the chopped dill and serve.

Pita Brittle

SERVES 6

SODIUM PER SERVING: 2 MG
CALORIES PER SERVING: 115

Pita brittle can be served by itself as a snack, or with drinks, with salads, with hot or cold soups, or as crackers with spreads. Any dried or fresh herb can be substituted for the oregano. Leftover pita brittle will keep well if it is stored in a tightly covered jar in the refrigerator. Reheat it before serving. This recipe is easily doubled or halved to suit the number of people being served.

3 whole salt-free pita bread rounds
* or Indian Puffed Bread (see page 141)*
¼ cup melted unsalted butter
3 tablespoons dried oregano

Preheat the oven to 250°F.

Cut each bread round into two halves. With a pastry brush, spread melted butter evenly over each round. Sprinkle with oregano.

Place the rounds on ungreased baking sheets and bake until golden brown, about 1 hour.

Break the rounds into bite-size pieces. Serve warm.

Marinated Mushrooms

SERVES 4

SODIUM PER SERVING: 20 MG
CALORIES PER SERVING: 222

Serve these mushrooms on toothpicks with drinks or as a first course on a bed of lettuce. For variety, forest mushrooms such as shiitake or golden oak can be used, but before marinating they should be blanched or sautéed in vegetable oil until soft.

1 pound fresh white mushrooms
1 tablespoon lemon juice
½ cup Vinaigrette (see page 20)
1 tablespoon lemon juice
1 small sweet red pepper, seeded and cut into strips
1 to 2 tablespoons chopped fresh herbs, such as tarragon,
* coriander, marjoram, dill, parsley, or chives*

Rinse the mushrooms and gently wipe dry with paper towels. Trim the stems. Slice the mushrooms about ¼-inch thick. Leave tiny mushrooms whole. Put the mushrooms into a serving dish and sprinkle with the lemon juice.

Pour the vinaigrette over the mushrooms. Marinate for not more than 2 hours.

Before serving, drain off any excess vinaigrette. Garnish with the strips of red pepper and sprinkle with the chopped herbs.

Fresh Mozzarella, Tomato, and Basil

SERVES 4

SODIUM PER SERVING: 29 MG
CALORIES PER SERVING: 447

Ripe tomatoes, fresh basil, and mozzarella cheese are a marriage made in heaven. This dish is particularly good as a first course for a summer lunch or dinner. Fresh, unsalted mozzarella is available in many super-markets and most Italian delicatessens.

2 large, ripe beefsteak tomatoes
½ pound fresh unsalted mozzarella cheese
1 sweet onion, thinly sliced
6 tablespoons olive oil
2 tablespoons wine vinegar
½ teaspoon finely chopped garlic
freshly ground black pepper
¼ cup chopped fresh basil

Slice the tomatoes and mozarella thickly.

On individual plates arrange alternating slices of tomato, mozzarella, and onion.

In a small bowl combine the oil, vinegar, garlic, and black pepper. Whisk with a fork until well blended. Correct the seasoning to taste.

Still whisking with the fork, pour the dressing evenly over each plate. Garnish with the chopped basil.

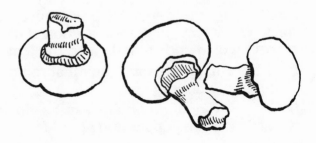

Stuffed Mushrooms in Foil

SERVES 4

SODIUM PER SERVING: 9 MG
CALORIES PER SERVING: 39

Served as a first course, or as a side dish, these stuffed mushrooms are always impressive. They can be cooked in the oven or on an outdoor grill.

8 large mushrooms
2 garlic cloves
4 teaspoons chopped fresh parsley
2 teaspoons olive oil
½ cup chopped onion
1 teaspoon dried whole-leaf thyme
freshly ground black pepper

Preheat the oven to 425ºF. If cooking outdoors, use white coals.

Rinse the mushrooms and gently wipe dry with paper towels. Remove the stems and trim off the ends.

Coarsely chop the mushroom stems, garlic and parsley.

Heat the olive oil in a large skillet. Add the onion and thyme and sauté over medium-high heat for 7 minutes, stirring frequently. Add the chopped mushroom stem mixture and black pepper to taste. Cook for 5 minutes more.

Divide the onion mixture into eight equal parts and stuff the mushroom caps. Place the stuffed mushrooms caps on a piece of aluminum foil large enough to form a package around them. Wrap the foil around the mushrooms, folding the ends over each other to form a leakproof seam. Cook for 12 to 15 minutes.

Open the package carefully. Spoon the juices over the mushrooms and serve.

Chopped Chicken Livers

SERVES 6

SODIUM PER SERVING: 66 MG
CALORIES PER SERVING: 181

The apples, cinnamon, and nutmeg add texture and spice to this
version of a favorite family recipe. It is particularly good when served
as an appetizer before a main course of fish.

2 tablespoons vegetable oil
1 medium-sized onion, sliced
4 shallots, diced
2 garlic cloves, minced
¾ pound fresh chicken livers
2 tart apples, peeled, cored, and thickly sliced
2 hard-cooked eggs, peeled
¼ teaspoon ground cinnamon
¼ teaspoon ground nutmeg
freshly ground black pepper

Heat the oil in a large, heavy skillet over medium heat.
Add the onion, shallots, and garlic. Cook until soft, stirring
frequently with a wooden spoon. Move the onion mixture to
one side of the pan. Add the chicken livers. Cook the livers
until they are firm and the pink juices have stopped running.
This will take about 6 minutes per side.

Add the apple slices to the pan. Gently mix all the ingredients. Continue to cook until the apple slices begin to soften.
Remove the skillet from the heat and let the ingredients cool.

Put the liver mixture into the bowl of a food processor.
Add the eggs, cinnamon, nutmeg, and black pepper to taste.
Using the metal blade, with an on-off motion process until
the mixture is coarsely chopped. Alternatively, finely chop
the liver mixture with a chopping blade in a wooden bowl
or with a heavy knife on a chopping board.

Chill until 30 minutes before serving.

Soups

Making a good soup is probably the greatest challenge of salt-free cooking. It requires a blend of good basic ingredients, herbs, and spices to make a good salt-free stock that has body and depth of flavor. Often the soup starts with a larger quantity of basic ingredients and is cooked or cooled longer to further concentrate the flavors. These flavorful stocks can easily be made in large batches, divided into smaller quantities, and frozen for later use. They're well worth the effort. With stock in the freezer, a solid base for improvising any hot or chilled soup is readily available. Good stock is also the base of many sauces.

When making any soup, always skim the foam off the top as it cooks. This will make the soup clearer and more appetizing. Strain stock through a sieve lined with clean cheesecloth. Remove as much fat as possible from meat soups before serving.

Not all the recipes in this chapter require stock for the base. Although every soup will have a richer flavor if it is made with stock, Curried Split Pea Soup, Gazpacho, Chilled Cucumber Soup, and Watercress and Potato Soup are among those that can be made with other liquids.

No food is more satisfying than a steaming bowl of hot soup on a cold day. On a warm day, a refreshingly cold soup is just as welcome. A hot or a cold soup served with a simple green salad and crusty bread becomes a meal in itself. We like to ladle soup from a handsome soup tureen into soup bowls at the table.

Vegetable Stock

MAKES 3½ QUARTS

SODIUM PER RECIPE: LESS THAN 0.5 MG
CALORIES PER RECIPE: LESS THAN 5

Basic vegetable stock can be substituted for chicken or beef broth or stock in almost any recipe. Strain the stock before using it as a base for vegetable soup. This stock freezes well.

2 tablespoons olive oil
1 whole large leek, coarsely chopped
1 medium-sized onion, coarsely chopped
1 celery stalk, coarsely chopped (optional)
1 large parsnip, peeled and coarsely chopped
2 carrots, peeled and coarsely chopped
4 garlic cloves, crushed
½ cup chopped fresh parsley
½ teaspoon dried whole-leaf thyme
4 quarts water
2 bay leaves
10 black peppercorns
¼ teaspoon dill seeds
freshly ground black pepper to taste
1 large potato, quartered

Heat the olive oil in a large, heavy pot. Add the leek, onion, celery, parsnip, carrots, garlic, parsley and thyme. Sauté, stirring frequently, for 15 minutes, or until the vegetables are soft and golden.

Add the water, bay leaves, peppercorns, dill seeds, black pepper, and potato. Simmer, partially covered, for 2 hours.

Remove the potato quarters from the stock. Peel the quarters and mash the potato in a small bowl. Slowly stir in enough stock from the pot to make the potato liquid. Pour the liquid back into the pot and cook 15 minutes longer. Omit this step if you want a clearer stock.

Remove the pot from the heat and let the stock cool for 1 to 2 hours. Strain the broth and discard the solids.

Fish Stock

MAKES 3 QUARTS

SODIUM PER RECIPE: LESS THAN 0.5 MG
CALORIES PER RECIPE: LESS THAN 5

This stock is an excellent base for fish soups and stews — or you can serve it as is, garnished with a sprig of parsley or thyme.

5 pounds fresh fish bones and heads
3 quarts water
2 cups white wine
2 carrots, peeled and quartered
4 bay leaves
2 teaspoons dried whole-leaf thyme
2 garlic cloves, crushed
1 large sweet onion, sliced
6 parsley sprigs
1 tablespoon whole black peppercorns
2 tablespoons anise-flavored liqueur (optional)

Put the fish, water, wine, carrots, bay leaves, thyme, garlic, onion, parsley and peppercorns into a large heavy pot. Bring to a boil, partially cover the pot, reduce the heat, and simmer gently for 30 minutes. Skim the top occasionally as the stock cooks.

Strain the stock, discarding the solids.
Return the stock to the pot and add the anise-flavored liqueur. Simmer for 30 minutes more. Cool. Store well covered in the refrigerator or freeze for future use.

Chicken Stock

MAKES 1¼ QUARTS

SODIUM PER RECIPE: LESS THAN 0.5 MG
CALORIES PER RECIPE: LESS THAN 5

The full flavor of this soup often surprises people who insist that chicken soup must be made with salt. When serving the soup, add some cooked rice or thin egg noodles, some of the cooked carrots, and a sprig of parsley. For a main course, or chicken in the pot, cut the leftover chicken into eighths. Put the pieces into large, deep soup plates, add the cooked vegetables and cooked noodles or rice, and top with the soup.

4 whole cloves
1 large onion, halved
8 parsley sprigs
4 dill sprigs
2 whole leeks, halved lengthwise
1 large chicken, quartered, with giblets (except liver)
1 parsnip, peeled
2 carrots, peeled and halved
2 quarts water
8 black peppercorns

Stick 2 cloves into each onion half. Tie the parsley, dill and leeks together with butcher's string or heavy white sewing thread.

Put the onions, parsley, dill, leeks, chicken, parsnip, carrots, water, and peppercorns into a large heavy pot. Bring to a boil and skim the surface. Cover the pot, reduce the heat, and simmer for 1 hour.

Let the soup cool, covered, for 1 hour. Remove the vegetables and chicken pieces and reserve. Skim again with a slotted spoon to remove fat.

Line a large strainer with cheesecloth or a white linen napkin. Strain the soup into another pot. Reheat and serve or refrigerate for later use.

Oyster Soup

SERVES 4

SODIUM PER SERVING: 103 MG
CALORIES PER SERVING: 194

A steaming bowl of oysters in clear broth is a welcome start to a meal on a cool day. The crispness and bright color of the carrot contrast nicely with the delicate oysters.

2 tablespoons olive oil
1 green pepper, seeded and chopped
1 whole leek, chopped
1 medium-sized onion, chopped
3 cups Fish Stock (see page 49)
½ cup dry white wine
1 tablespoon lemon juice
1 pint (about 2½ cups) shucked oysters with their liquid
½ teaspoon dried whole-leaf thyme
⅛ teaspoon hot red pepper flakes
1 small carrot, peeled and julienned

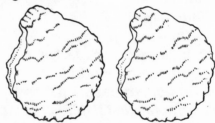

Heat the oil in a skillet. Add the green pepper, leek, and onion. Sauté over medium heat until the vegetables are soft.

With a slotted spoon, transfer the vegetables to a large pot. Add the fish stock, wine, and lemon juice. Bring the mixture to a boil. Reduce the heat and simmer, uncovered, until the flavors are well blended, about 7 minutes.

Add the oysters and their liquid, the thyme, and the red pepper flakes. Continue to simmer until the edges of the oysters are slightly curled, about 5 minutes.

With a slotted spoon, remove the oysters and put them into four individual soup bowls. Spoon the broth over the oysters.

Garnish with the julienned carrots and serve immediately.

Fisherman's Soup

SERVES 6

SODIUM PER SERVING: 94 MG
CALORIES PER SERVING: 248

Almost any fish, including haddock, tilefish, and snapper, may be used
for this full-bodied soup. For a spicier version, add some hot red pepper
flakes or a few dashes of hot pepper sauce. A spoonful of Pernod or a
pinch of saffron will add even more flavor. For a heartier soup, add a cup
of broken spaghetti pieces along with the tomatoes.

2 tablespoons olive oil
1 large onion, sliced
2 garlic cloves, finely chopped
6 parsley sprigs
1 green pepper, seeded and diced
1 28-ounce can salt-free crushed tomatoes
10 whole black peppercorns
2 bay leaves
½ teaspoons dried whole-leaf thyme
½ teaspoon sugar
⅓ cup white wine
1 tablespoon lemon juice
2 cups Fish Stock (see page 49)
1 tablespoon Pernod (optional)
¼ teaspoon hot red pepper flakes (optional)
2 pounds firm-fleshed fish fillets, cut into 1-inch pieces
3 tablespoons chopped parsley

Heat the olive oil in a large, heavy pot over medium heat.
Add the onion, garlic, and parsley. Cook, stirring frequently,
until the onions are soft, about 5 minutes. Add the green
pepper and cook, stirring frequently, until it starts to soften,
about 5 minutes more. Add the crushed tomatoes, peppercorns, bay leaves, thyme, sugar, white wine, lemon juice,
fish stock, Pernod and red pepper flakes. Mix well. Simmer,
uncovered, for 15 minutes.

Add the fish to the pot. Simmer only until the fish flakes
easily, about 7 to 10 minutes longer. Serve hot in deep bowls
garnished with the chopped parsley.

Curried Split Pea Soup

SERVES 6

SODIUM PER SERVING: 49 MG
CALORIES PER SERVING: 263

This is an unusually satisfying version of split pea soup.

2 cups dried split green peas
2 quarts water or Vegetable Stock (see page 48)
8 dried Oriental mushrooms
1 onion, coarsely chopped
1 large carrot, coarsely chopped
2 garlic cloves, halved
1½ tablespoons chopped fresh ginger
2 teaspoons curry powder
6 tablespoons unflavored low-fat yogurt
chopped chives or coriander

Rinse and pick over the split peas. Soak them overnight in the water or vegetable stock in a large pot. The next day, bring the liquid to a boil over moderate heat. Cover the pot and remove from the heat. Let stand for 1 hour.

Soak the mushrooms in 1 cup of warm water until softened, about 20 minutes. Strain and reserve the liquid. Cut away and discard the tough stems of the mushrooms. Coarsely chop the mushrooms.

Return the pot with the split peas to the heat. Add the reserved mushroom liquid, the mushrooms, and the onion, carrot and garlic. Stir in the ginger and curry powder. Cover the pot and simmer over medium heat until the peas are tender, about 45 minutes.

Remove the pot from the heat and let the soup cool slightly. Purée the soup in the container of a food processor or blender, or in a food mill or by pressing the soup through a sieve.

Serve hot or chilled, garnished with the yogurt and chopped chives or coriander.

Watercress and Potato Soup

SERVES 6

SODIUM PER SERVING: 45 MG
CALORIES PER SERVING: 145

This is an all-season soup that can be served hot in cold weather and cold in hot weather. The refreshing, peppery flavor of the watercress adds zing to the potatoes. Serve the soup with crisp sesame bread sticks and follow it with a hearty salad or simple poached fish or chicken.

1½ tablespoons unsalted butter
3 whole scallions, minced
1 carrot, peeled and grated
3½ cups Vegetable Stock (see page 48)
3 large Idaho potatoes, peeled and cut into ½-inch slices
1 cup chopped watercress, tough stems removed
½ cup unflavored low-fat yogurt
½ cup low-fat milk
freshly ground black pepper
6 watercress sprigs

Melt the butter in a larger, heavy pot over low heat. Add the scallions and carrot. Cover the pot and cook until the vegetables are very soft, about 5 to 8 minutes. Add the potatoes and stock to the pot. Cover, raise heat to medium, and cook until the potatoes are tender, about 20 minutes.

Purée the contents of the pot in batches in a blender or food processor. Return the mixture to the pot and stir in the watercress, yogurt, milk, and black pepper to taste. To make the soup by hand, remove the vegetables from the liquid with a slotted spoon. Put them in a small bowl and mash them. Return the mashed vegetables to the soup and blend well. Add the remaining ingredients.

Simmer gently for 10 minutes to blend the flavors.

Serve hot or cold, garnished with the watercress sprigs.

Craig Claiborne's Potage Arlèsienne

SERVES 6 TO 8

SODIUM PER SERVING: 27 MG
CALORIES PER SERVING: 206

Craig Claiborne, Food Editor of *The New York Times*, is the author of many fine cookbooks, including *The New* New York Times *Cookbook* and *Craig Claiborne's Gourmet Diet Cookbook*. In addition, he is a delightful host and friend.

¼ cup vegetable oil
1 1-pound eggplant, peeled and cut into small cubes
3 tablespoons unsalted butter
1¾ cups chopped onions
1 tablespoon finely minced garlic
freshly ground black pepper
1 bay leaf
¾ teaspoon dried whole-leaf thyme
3 cups salt-free canned tomatoes
¼ cup uncooked rice
4 cups salt-free chicken broth

Heat the oil in a large skillet. When it is very hot, add the eggplant cubes. Cook, shaking the skillet and stirring frequently, until the cubes are lightly browned. Remove the cubes from the skillet with a slotted spoon and drain them in a colander. There should be about 2¼ cups.

Heat the butter in a large saucepan. Add the onions and garlic. Cook, stirring constantly, until they are wilted. Add the eggplant, black pepper to taste, the bay leaf and thyme. Cook, stirring frequently, for 1 minute. Add the tomatoes and stir well.

Add the rice and chicken broth and bring the soup to a boil. Cook, stirring frequently, for 30 minutes.

Remove the saucepan from the heat. Discard the bay leaf. In a food processor or blender, process the soup (in batches if necessary) until smooth.

Return the soup to the saucepan and bring it to the boil. Serve immediately.

Beet and Cabbage Soup

SERVES 4 TO 6

SODIUM PER SERVING: 47 MG
CALORIES PER SERVING: 73

Also known as borscht, beet and cabbage soup can be made into
a meat soup by substituting meat broth for the vegetable stock, red
wine for the white wine and adding a cup of cubed cooked beef. Either
way, it is a hearty dish. It is traditionally served with dark bread and
steamed small whole potatoes.

1½ cups shredded cabbage
1 cup thinly sliced onion
6 cups Vegetable Stock (see page 48)
2 cups julienned cooked beets
¾ cup white wine
chopped fresh dill, for garnish
unflavored low-fat yogurt, for garnish

Put the cabbage and onion into a larger, heavy saucepan.
Cover and cook the vegetables over medium heat in their
own liquid until tender, about 15 minutes. Shake the saucepan frequently to avoid burning.

Add the stock and the wine. Bring to a boil and reduce
heat to low. Add the beets and mix well. Continue to
cook until the beets are just heated through. Remove the
saucepan from the heat. Serve the soup hot or cold. Garnish
each serving with a spoonful of yogurt and a lot of dill.

Summer Vegetable Soup

SERVES 6

SODIUM PER SERVING: 2 MG
CALORIES PER SERVING: 55

Flecked with fresh basil and highlighted with uncooked tomatoes, this is
a delightful soup for a summer day. For a light supper, serve with cheese
and crackers, Coarse Sweet Mustard (see page 24), Apple Ginger Chutney
(see page 32) and Paula's Quick Onion Relish (see page 26). For a more
filling soup, add one cup of cooked shell beans.

4 cups Vegetable Stock (see page 00), chilled
1 cup cooked green beans, cut into 1-inch pieces
1½ cup cooked corn kernels
1 tablespoon red wine vinegar
1 teaspoon extra-virgin olive oil
1 cup ripe plum tomatoes, cut into 1-inch pieces and seeded
½ cup coarsely chopped basil leaves

Pour the vegetable stock into a large serving bowl.
Add the green beans, corn, wine vinegar, and olive oil.
Mix well. Immediately before serving, add the tomatoes
and the basil. Serve cold or at room temperature.

Chilled Yogurt Soup

SERVES 4

SODIUM PER SERVING: 48 MG
CALORIES PER SERVING: 49

Delightful on a hot day, this simple soup requires no cooking.
The cayenne pepper adds bite and a dash of color.

1 cucumber, peeled, seeded, and cut into 2-inch pieces
1 tomato, seeded and chopped
3 tablespoons chopped sweet onion
2 tablespoons chopped fresh mint, chives and/or dill
1 cup unflavored low-fat yogurt
½ teaspoon ground cumin
6 mint sprigs
cayenne pepper

Put the cucumber, tomato, onion and herb(s) into the
container of a food processor or blender. Process until very
fine. Add the yogurt and cumin and blend well. To make by
hand, chop the cucumber, onion and herb(s) finely, reserving
as much liquid as possible. Put the chopped ingredients
and any reserved liquid into a mixing bowl and add the
remaining ingredients.

Serve chilled, garnished with a sprig of mint and a sprinkling
of cayenne to taste.

Gazpacho

SERVES 6

SODIUM PER SERVING: 13 MG
CALORIES PER SERVING: 83

Gazpacho is a summer favorite. Tomatoes are the main ingredient, but the quantities given here are just a guide. You can vary the amounts of the other vegetables to taste.

2 pounds ripe tomatoes, blanched, peeled, seeded, and coarsely chopped
1 cucumber, peeled, seeded, and coarsely chopped
4 tablespoons chopped parsley leaves (no stems)
1 green pepper, seeded and coarsely chopped
1 medium-sized sweet onion, coarsely chopped
1 garlic clove, coarsely chopped
1 12-ounce can salt-free tomato juice
1 tablespoon olive oil
1 tablespoon wine vinegar
2 tablespoons lemon juice
¼ teaspoon cayenne pepper
freshly ground black pepper

Reserve ¼ cup each of the tomatoes and cucumber and 1 tablespoon of the chopped parsley.

Put the remaining tomatoes, cucumber and parsley and the green pepper, onion, garlic, tomato juice, olive oil, vinegar, lemon juice, cayenne pepper and black pepper to taste in batches into the container of a blender or food processor. Purée until smooth. Combine the batches in a large serving bowl. (To make gazpacho by hand, chop the vegetables as finely as possible and put them into a large serving bowl). Add the remaining ingredients and mix well.

Chill 1 to 2 hours before serving. Garnish with the reserved tomatoes, cucumber and parsley. Serve cold.

Salads

The wide variety of greens and fresh herbs available year round makes for salads that are full of color, texture, and flavor. In the lettuce family alone, a well-stocked market will have romaine, red and green leaf lettuce, chicory, escarole, Boston lettuce, and the ubiquitous iceberg lettuce. In addition, endive, watercress, and dandelion greens, and such fresh herbs as parsley, basil, mint, and coriander, are easily found. And when something interesting turns up, like raddichio (rocket), try it.

A good green salad should include at least two greens and one fresh herb, but beyond that, no recipe is really required. A green salad is best when it is simply dressed with a vinaigrette made with the best possible oil and vinegar. A recipe for basic vinaigrette is given on page 20. Recipes for oil-free dressings are on page 21.

The recipes in this chapter are for salads that are not based primarily on greens. Some, such as Potato Salad with White Wine Dressing, are new versions of traditional salads. Others, such as Tiny Potatoes and Minted Pea Pods, are original — and delicious.

Rice Salad

SERVES 4

SODIUM PER SERVING: 12 MG
CALORIES PER SERVING: 184

So that the flavors blend well, make this salad while the rice is still warm. In addition to or instead of the vegetables used in this recipe, try additional diced cucumbers or seeded tomatoes, diced cooked meat or seafood, such diced fruits as apple, orange, and pineapple, or toasted almonds or pine nuts.

2 cups cooked rice
4 tablespoons Vinaigrette (see page 20)
2 tablespoons lemon juice
1 green or sweet red pepper, finely diced
3 whole scallions, chopped
1 carrot, peeled and finely diced
3 tablespoons chopped parsley, dill or basil
freshly ground black pepper

Put the rice into a serving bowl and pour the vinaigrette and lemon juice over it. Toss well with a fork. Add the peppers, scallions, carrot, chopped herbs and black pepper to taste. Mix well and let cool. Serve at room temperature.

Potato Salad with White Wine Dressing

SERVES 8

SODIUM PER SERVING: 40 MG
CALORIES PER SERVING: 175

The low-fat yogurt, mustard, and white wine combine to make
a low-calorie, low-cholesterol dressing that has an elegant flavor.
Tarragon- or any herb-flavored vinegar can be substituted for the wine.

6 medium-sized russet potatoes
1½ green peppers, chopped
1½ sweet red peppers, chopped
4 whole scallions, chopped
1 cup unflavored low-fat yogurt
½ cup salt-free Dijon-style mustard
¼ cup white wine
freshly ground black pepper

Put the potatoes into a large saucepan. Add water to cover
and boil for 25 minutes, or until the potatoes can just be
easily pierced with a fork. Immediately drain the potatoes
and rinse under cold water.

Peel and slice the potatoes while they are still warm.
Put slices into a serving bowl.

In a small bowl, combine the green and red peppers,
scallions, yogurt, mustard, wine, tarragon, and black
pepper. Whisk well to blend. Pour the dressing over the
warm, sliced potatoes and mix gently but well.
The warm potatoes will absorb the flavors of the
dressing. Serve at room temperature.

Coleslaw with Yogurt Dressing

SERVES 8

SODIUM PER SERVING: 55 MG
CALORIES PER SERVING: 88

To make coleslaw for four people, simply cut this recipe in half.
This salad is a favorite for picnics and barbecues.

1 medium-sized head green cabbage, cored and shredded
2 carrots, peeled and thinly sliced
1 green pepper, thinly sliced

Dressing:
⅓ cup sugar
⅓ cup white vinegar
1½ cup unflavored low-fat yogurt
freshly ground black pepper

Put the cabbage, carrots, and green pepper
into a serving bowl.
In a small bowl, dissolve the sugar in the vinegar.
Mix well, using a fork or small whisk. Add the yogurt and
mix until well blended. Add black pepper to taste.
Pour the dressing over the vegetables and toss well. Let the
coleslaw stand for 30 minutes to allow the flavors to blend.
Serve at room temperature.

Barbara Kafka's Mixed Vegetable Salad

SERVES 6 TO 8

SODIUM PER SERVING: 77 MG
CALORIES PER SERVING: 307

The author of several cookbooks, food consultant and food editor of
Vogue magazine, Barbara Kafka has an extraordinary knowledge of
food and wine. Low-fat yogurt may be substituted for the sour cream.

2 cucumbers, peeled, seeded, and diced
2 large, ripe tomatoes, seeded and diced
1 sweet red pepper, seeded and diced
1 green pepper, seeded and diced
2 bunches fresh dill, coarsely chopped
1 bunch scallions (white parts only), chopped
4 cups sour cream
2 tablespoons fresh lemon juice
freshly ground black pepper to taste
hot red pepper flakes to taste (optional)

Put all the ingredients into a large serving bowl. Mix well.
Chill for 1 hour and serve.

Grated Carrot Salad

SERVES 6

SODIUM PER SERVING: 29 MG
CALORIES PER SERVING: 111

This crunchy, refreshing salad is easily made any time of the year.

¾ pound carrots, peeled and coarsely grated
½ cup sweet onion, finely chopped

Dressing:

¼ cup olive oil
1 tablespoon lemon juice
1 tablespoon wine vinegar
freshly ground black pepper
1 tablespoon fresh mint, finely chopped
*   or ½ teaspoon dried mint, crumbled*
½ teaspoon cumin seed

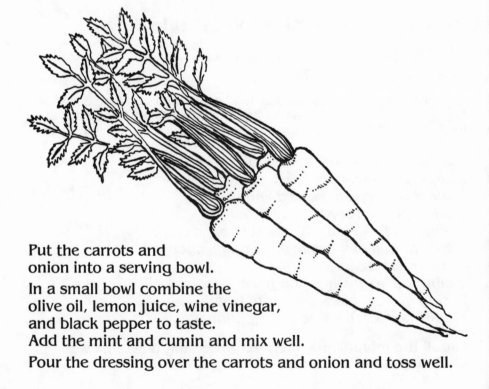

Put the carrots and
onion into a serving bowl.

In a small bowl combine the
olive oil, lemon juice, wine vinegar,
and black pepper to taste.
Add the mint and cumin and mix well.

Pour the dressing over the carrots and onion and toss well.

Citrus and Onion Salad

SERVES 4

SODIUM PER SERVING: 14 MG
CALORIES PER SERVING: 187

Oranges and onions are a refreshing combination for a salad.
For a heartier salad, add some avocado slices.

1 small head green leaf or romaine lettuce
1 bunch watercress
3 navel oranges
½ medium-sized sweet onion
3 tablespoons chopped fresh parsley or chives

Dressing:

4 tablespoons olive oil
1 to 2 tablespoons red wine vinegar
1 tablespoon orange juice
freshly ground black pepper

Thoroughly wash and dry the lettuce and watercress.
Tear the lettuce into bite-sized pieces. Remove the tough
stems from the watercress. Make a bed of lettuce and
watercress on a serving platter.

Peel the oranges, removing as much of the white pith as
possible. Slice the oranges into ½-inch rounds, then cut the
rounds in half and put them into a bowl.

Slice the onion very thinly. Place the slices in the bowl
with the oranges and add the chopped herbs. Toss gently
but well. Arrange the orange and onion slices on the bed of
lettuce and watercress.

In a small bowl, combine the olive oil, vinegar, orange juice
and black pepper to taste. Whisk well.

Pour the dressing over the salad and serve.

Fennel Salad

SERVES 4

SODIUM PER SERVING: 7 MG
CALORIES PER SERVING: 150

Fennel is a delicious vegetable with an aniselike flavor. It is a good, low-sodium substitute for celery in soups and stews. Fennel is good sautéed, braised, or used in salads.

1 large fennel bulb
1 pint very small cherry tomatoes

Dressing:

½ teaspoon minced garlic
freshly ground black pepper
1 tablespoon red wine vinegar
2 teaspoons lemon juice
4 tablespoons olive oil

Remove the feathers (leaves) from the fennel bulb, reserving a few for garnish. Wash and trim the bulb, then quarter it. Cut each quarter crosswise into thin slices. Put the fennel slices into a shallow salad bowl.

Trim the cherry tomatoes and add them to the salad bowl.

To make the dressing, put the garlic and black pepper to taste into a small bowl. Add the vinegar and lemon juice and stir well. Whisk in the olive oil.

Pour the dressing over the fennel and tomatoes and toss well. Garnish with some fennel leaves and serve.

Beefsteak Tomatoes
with Brandy Basil Dressing

SERVES 4 TO 6

SODIUM PER SERVING: 3 MG
CALORIES PER SERVING: 133

The brandy in the dressing adds a delightful flavor that perfectly complements the luscious flavor of the ripe tomatoes.

2 tablespoons brandy
4 tablespoons olive oil
½ cup chopped fresh basil
freshly ground black pepper
2 large, ripe beefsteak tomatoes, thickly sliced

Put the brandy, olive oil, basil and black pepper to taste into a jar with a tightly fitting lid. Shake well.

Arrange the tomato slices on a serving plate.
Pour the dressing over them and serve.

Cucumber Raita

SERVES 4

SODIUM PER SERVING: 45 MG
CALORIES PER SERVING: 48

Serve this Indian yogurt-based salad with grilled meat, fish or poultry or as a soothing complement to spicy foods.

2 cucumbers, peeled, seeded, and diced
2 to 3 tablespoons diced sweet onion (optional)
1 cup unflavored low-fat yogurt
½ teaspoon ground cumin
2 tablespoons chopped fresh coriander or mint
cayenne pepper (optional)

In a serving bowl, toss the cucumber and onion with the yogurt, cumin and coriander or mint. Serve chilled, garnished with a sprig of coriander or mint and a sprinkle of cayenne pepper if desired.

Asparagus in Vinaigrette

SERVES 6

SODIUM PER SERVING: 3 MG
CALORIES PER SERVING: 133

This dish makes a good first course. It's also good as an accompaniment to a main dish such as Chicken and Dumplings (see page 104). Serve it in individual small dishes.

1½ pounds asparagus
5 tablespoons olive oil
1 tablespoon wine vinegar
1 tablespoon lemon juice
2 tablespoons finely chopped shallots
freshly ground black pepper
2 tablespoons chopped parsley

Wash the asparagus and cut off the tough stems. Peel the stalks with a swivel peeler if desired. Cut the asparagus diagonally into 2-inch pieces.

Pour enough water into a large skillet to fill it to a depth of 1 inch. Bring the water to a boil, add the asparagus pieces, and cover the skillet. Cook until the asparagus are tender, about 5 minutes. Drain the asparagus well and transfer to a serving dish.

To prepare the vinaigrette, in a small bowl mix the oil, vinegar, lemon juice, shallot and black pepper to taste. Mix well.

Pour the vinaigrette over the warm asparagus and toss well. Let stand for 30 minutes to allow the flavors to blend. Sprinkle with chopped parsley and serve at room temperature.

Yam and Apple Salad

SERVES 6

SODIUM PER SERVING: 32 MG
CALORIES PER SERVING: 243

Yams are a darker orange color than sweet potatoes and are somewhat more moist. They are an excellent source of Vitamin A.

4 medium yams or sweet potatoes
½ tart apple, cored and thinly sliced
½ cup red cabbage, coarsely chopped
½ cup roasted, unsalted peanuts
2 whole small scallions, sliced

Dressing:

½ cup orange juice
⅔ cup unflavored low-fat yogurt
1½ tablespoons lemon juice

Cook the yams in boiling water to cover until they are just tender, about 25 minutes. Drain the yams and rinse them under cold water. When the yams are cool enough to handle, peel them, then slice them into ¼-inch rounds.

Put the sliced yams, apple, cabbage, peanuts, and scallions into a serving bowl.

In a small bowl, combine the orange juice, yogurt, and lemon juice. Blend well and pour over the ingredients in the serving bowl. Toss well and serve.

Lentil Salad

SERVES 6

SODIUM PER SERVING: 12 MG
CALORIES PER SERVING: 235

This basic recipe can be enhanced with chopped, seeded tomatoes, crumbled, mild goat cheese, diced cucumbers, or walnut halves.

1 cup dried lentils
1 garlic clove, minced
freshly ground black pepper
1 tablespoon lemon juice
1 tablespoon wine vinegar
6 tablespoons olive oil
3 tablespoons chopped fresh parsley or mint
½ cup sweet onion, chopped
zest of 1 lemon

Put the lentils into a saucepan with 3 cups of water. Bring to a boil, cover the saucepan, and lower the heat. Simmer until the lentils are tender, about 35 to 45 minutes. Check often during the last 10 minutes of cooking to avoid overcooking. Drain the lentils well and put them into a serving bowl.

In a small bowl, mash the garlic with black pepper to taste. Add the lemon juice and vinegar. With a fork or small whisk, blend in the olive oil. Add the parsley or mint and the onion and mix well.

Pour the dressing over the lentils and toss well. Sprinkle the lemon zest over the top. Refrigerate for about 3 hours. Remove from the refrigerator 30 minutes before serving.

Tiny Potatoes and Minted Pea Pods

SERVES 6

SODIUM PER SERVING: 5 MG
CALORIES PER SERVING: 178

Ideally, this salad should be made with freshly dug, tiny new potatoes. If new potatoes are not available, substitute the same amount of thin-skinned mature potatoes. Peel the potatoes and use a melon baller to scoop them into small balls. Cook the potato balls until they are just tender and proceed with the recipe.

1 ½ pounds tiny new potatoes (¾ inch in diameter)
¼ pound fresh snow peas or sugar snap peas
4 tablespoons safflower oil
1 tablespoon lemon juice
1 teaspoon white wine vinegar
freshly ground black pepper
1 tablespoon finely chopped fresh mint
2 tablespoons coarsely chopped chives

Gently scrub the potatoes. Cook them in boiling water until just tender, about 15 minutes. Be careful not to overcook them. Drain the potatoes well and place them in a serving bowl.

Slice the pea pods diagonally into pieces 1 ½ inches long.

In a small bowl, combine the oil, lemon juice, vinegar, and black pepper to taste. Mix well and pour over the potatoes. Add the pea pods, mint and chives, and toss gently. Serve warm or at room temperature.

Fish

Today, the main dish at many an elegant dinner party is fish. It's hardly surprising — fish is low in cholesterol and calories, but high in protein and versatility.

Whether you're poaching, steaming, broiling, grilling, roasting, or sautéeing your fish, and whether it's being served hot or cold, in a soup or in a salad, use the freshest fish possible. Be sure the fish is odor-free, without any "fishy" smell. The skin should be shiny, not dull-looking, and the flesh should be firm to the touch and spring back when pressed.

A general rule for cooking a whole fish is to measure the thickness of the fish behind the head and then allow eight to nine minutes cooking time for each inch of thickness. Fish is done when the meat becomes white or opaque and flakes easily with a fork. Never overcook fish.

The fish available in most fish markets fall into two categories: oily, including tuna, salmon, swordfish, mackerel, bluefish, and pompano; and lean, including cod, halibut, haddock, sole, flounder, sea bass, striped bass, whiting, pike, and red snapper.

Fish dishes are traditionally garnished with lemon or lime juice and wedges and/or chopped parsley or dill. Butter and white wine are often used in cooking. Thyme, grated ginger, and saffron may be used for special flavor.

Such shellfish as clams and mussels must, unfortunately, often be omitted from a medically restricted salt-free diet because of their naturally high sodium content. The exception is oysters, which are usually permissible.

Glazed Whole Baked Fish

SERVES 4

SODIUM PER SERVING: 66 MG
CALORIES PER SERVING: 455

This recipe works particularly well with porgy or red snapper. The bronzed, crispy skin glazed with chutney is a nice contrast to the soft, white fish.

1 4-pound or 2 2-pound whole firm-fleshed fish, cleaned, with head and tail

3 whole scallions, sliced lengthwise very thinly

1 tablespoon julienned ginger

2 garlic cloves, halved

2 tablespoons lemon juice

3 tablespoons Apple Ginger Chutney (see page 32)

2 tablespoons vegetable oil

Preheat the oven to 375°F. Coat with 1 tablespoon of oil the bottom of a baking dish that is as close to the size of the fish as possible.

Wash the fish and gently pat dry. Put the scallions, ginger, and garlic into the cavity of the fish.

Put the fish into the baking dish and sprinkle with the lemon juice. Coat the top of the fish with the chutney and then with the remaining 1 tablespoon of oil.

Bake the fish, basting occasionally with the pan drippings, until it is firm to the touch and the skin is golden brown, about 25 minutes. Serve immediately.

Broiled Fish Steaks with Green Peppercorns

SERVES 4

SODIUM PER SERVING: 62 MG
CALORIES PER SERVING: 152

Any firm-fleshed fish can be used for this recipe. Cod, halibut, swordfish, or tilefish are good choices. The green peppercorns add real zip.

1 tablespoon green peppercorns
1 tablespoon plus ½ teaspoon vegetable oil
3 tablespoons lemon juice
4 8-ounce fish steaks, each about 1 inch thick
lemon wedges

Rinse the green peppercorns in cold water and drain well. Put them into a small bowl and add 1 tablespoon of oil. With the back of a spoon, crush the green peppercorns into the oil. Add the lemon juice and mix well.

Put the fish steaks into a shallow dish. Pour the green peppercorn sauce over the steaks and marinate at room temperature for 30 to 60 minutes, turning the steaks occasionally.

Preheat the broiler to high. Brush the broiler pan lightly with the remaining ½ teaspoon of oil.

Broil the fish steaks 4 inches from the heat, brushing often with the marinade, until cooked through and opaque white in the center, about 10 minutes. The steaks do not have to be turned. Serve garnished with lemon wedges.

Barbecued Fish Steaks

SERVES 4

SODIUM PER SERVING: 199 MG
CALORIES PER SERVING: 378

This recipe works well with swordfish, halibut and, tuna. Save salmon steaks for a lighter sauce. Serve barbecued fish steaks with Grilled Vegetable Packets (see page 165) and Potato Salad with White Wine Dressing (see page 60) for an easy outdoor meal.

4 ¾-pound fish steaks, about 1 inch thick
1 cup Barbecue Sauce (see page 30)
vegetable oil

Gently pierce the fish steaks with a fork so that the sauce will penetrate. Put the fish steaks into a shallow dish and add the barbecue sauce. Marinate the steaks in the sauce, turning them occasionally, for 1 hour.

Preheat the broiler to high or prepare white coals.
Brush a broiling pan or grill with the oil.

Cook the fish steaks for 5 minutes on each side, brushing often with the barbecue sauce. Serve immediately.

Lime-Broiled Fish Steaks with Mustard and Ginger

SERVES 4

SODIUM PER SERVING: 124 MG
CALORIES PER SERVING: 287

Salmon, swordfish, halibut, and cod steaks are particularly good prepared this way. Try cooking them on an outdoor grill.

¼ cup lime juice
2 tablespoons vegetable oil
1 teaspoon salt-free Dijon-style mustard
2 teaspoons grated ginger
¼ teaspoon cayenne pepper
freshly ground black pepper
4 8-ounce fish steaks, each about 1 inch thick

In a bowl, combine the lime juice, 1 tablespoon of oil, ginger, cayenne pepper, and black pepper to taste.

Marinate the fish steaks in the marinade for 30 to 60 minutes, turning occasionally.

Preheat the broiler. Brush the broiler pan with the remaining oil. (If cooking outdoors, use white coals and brush the grill with the remaining oil.)

Broil the fish, brushing often with the marinade, until cooked through and opaque white in the center, about 10 minutes. Turn the fish after cooking for 5 minutes.

Poached Fish with Almonds

SERVES 4

SODIUM PER SERVING: 138 MG
CALORIES PER SERVING: 358

The toasted almonds give this delicately flavored dish color and crispness. Use fillets of scrod, sole, flounder, or red snapper. If you use frozen fillets, partially thaw them before cooking.

4 tablespoons unsalted butter
⅔ cup slivered, blanched almonds
¼ cup white wine
¼ cup lemon juice
½ cup water
¼ teaspoon white pepper
1½ pounds fish fillets

Melt the butter in a large heavy skillet. Add the almonds and sauté, stirring frequently, until they begin to turn golden. Remove the almonds with a slotted spoon and drain on paper towels. Set aside.

Add the wine, lemon juice, water and white pepper to the skillet. Stir well and bring to a simmer. Add the fish fillets and spoon the sauce over them.

Cover the skillet and gently poach the fillets until the fish flakes easily with a fork, about 7 to 8 minutes.

Place the fish on a serving platter. Spoon the sauce over the fillets and sprinkle with the almonds. Serve immediately.

Skillet-Steamed Fish

SERVES 4

SODIUM PER SERVING: 140 MG
CALORIES PER SERVING: 204

This is a never-fail recipe. Almost any fish can be prepared this way, particularly cleaned, small whole fish such as porgy, trout, and red snapper. Sole, flounder, scrod, haddock, and bluefish fillets are also good choices. If using frozen fish, partially thaw them first. To vary the recipe, try adding ½ teaspoon of hot red pepper flakes or a teaspoon or so of such chopped fresh herbs as dill, parsley, basil or thyme.

1 tablespoon vegetable oil
1 onion, coarsely chopped
1 garlic clove, crushed
2 large tomatoes, blanched, peeled, seeded,
    and coarsely chopped
2 tablespoons wine or cider vinegar
¾ cup water or Fish Stock (see page 49)
4 large fish fillets
freshly ground black pepper

Heat the oil in a large nonstick skillet over medium heat. Add the onion and garlic and cook, stirring frequently, until the onion is golden brown, about 5 minutes. Add the tomatoes. Stir well and cook until the tomatoes are just heated through, about 2 minutes. Add the vinegar and stir well.

Push the tomato mixture to one side of the skillet. Add the water or fish stock. When the liquid starts to simmer, add the fish and cover the skillet. Cook until the fish flakes easily, about 8 to 10 minutes.

Remove the fish and arrange on a serving platter. Add pepper to taste to the tomato mixture and stir. Spoon the tomato mixture over the fish. Serve immediately.

Oriental Steamed Whole Fish

SERVES 4

SODIUM PER SERVING: 48 MG
CALORIES PER SERVING: 305

As this dish proves, you can create an Oriental flavor without soy sauce. Any firm-fleshed whole fish, such as red snapper, pompano or striped bass can be used. Serve the fish with hot mustard on the side. It goes well with Broccoli with Dried Oriental Mushrooms (see page 148) and Noodles with Peanut Sauce (see page 128)

1 3-pound whole fish, cleaned
1 small bunch scallions, thinly julienned
2 tablespoons ginger root, slivered
1 tablespoon sesame oil
1 teaspoon sherry vinegar
3 tablespoons coriander leaves

Make 3 diagonal slashes on each side of the fish.

On a plate large enough to hold the whole fish, make a bed of half the scallions and ginger. Put the fish on top and drizzle the oil and vinegar over it. Cover the fish with the remaining scallions and ginger.

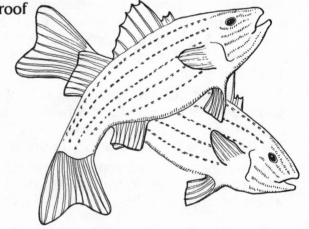

Invert a small, heatproof bowl that is about 4 inches deep and place it into the bottom of a pot large enough to hold the fish plate. Fill the pot with water to a depth of 2 inches.

Put the plate with the fish on the inverted bowl (the water should not touch the plate), cover the pot, and steam over medium-high heat until the fish is firm to the touch and flakes easily, about 8 to 10 minutes per inch of thickness. The water should boil for the entire time.

(A cooking rack that will hold the plate above the water may be used instead of an inverted bowl.)

Remove the plate from the steamer or pot. Spoon any liquid that has accumulated on the plate over the fish. Garnish with the coriander leaves and serve immediately.

Stir-Fried Fish Fillets with Leeks and Ginger

SERVES 4

SODIUM PER SERVING: 94 MG
CALORIES PER SERVING: 303

Stir-frying is a particularly good way to cook fish, since the quick cooking over high heat preserves the texture and fresh flavor of the fish. Serve this dish with Broccoli and Oranges in Vinaigrette (see page 149) or Sesame Green Beans (see page 144) and a simple rice pilaf.

4 tablespoons vegetable oil
1½ pounds fresh fish fillets, cut into 1-inch strips
2 large leeks, cut into thin, 2-inch strips
1 garlic clove, minced
1 tablespoon finely chopped fresh ginger
¼ teaspoon sugar
2 tablespoons sherry vinegar
2 tablespoons chopped coriander

Heat 2 tablespoons of the oil in a wok or large skillet over medium-high heat. When the oil is very hot, add the fish strips in small batches and cook, stirring constantly, until just cooked through, about 3 minutes per batch. Add additional oil if necessary. Remove each batch with a slotted spoon when done and set aside.

Add 2 tablespoons of the oil to the wok or skillet. When the oil is very hot, add the leeks, garlic, ginger, and sugar. Cook, stirring constantly, for 3 minutes. Add the sherry vinegar and cook, stirring constantly, for 1 minute longer. Return the cooked fish to the wok or skillet and cook, stirring gently, until heated through.

Arrange the mixture on a serving platter, sprinkle with the chopped coriander, and serve immediately.

Pierre Franey's Broiled Fish Steaks with Grapefruit

SERVES 4

SODIUM PER SERVING: 82 MG
CALORIES PER SERVING: 228

Pierre Franey is the author of several best-selling cookbooks, including *Pierre Franey's Low-Calorie Gourmet*. His popular weekly cooking column, "The Sixty-Minute Gourmet," is widely syndicated. He also collaborates with Craig Claiborne on weekly food features for *The New York Times Sunday Magazine*. For this recipe, he suggests using tilefish, cod, haddock, striped bass, grouper or red snapper.

2 teaspoons unsalted butter
2 large ripe grapefruits
2 tablespoons olive oil
1 teaspoon ground dried ginger
1 teaspoon dry mustard
1 teaspoon ground coriander
freshly ground black pepper
4 8-ounce fish steaks, skinned and boned
4 tablespoons chopped scallions

Grease a large baking dish with the butter.

Remove the skin from the grapefruits in the same way as peeling an apple. Start at the top of the grapefruit and cut in a circular fashion, removing the skin in one spiraling piece. Remove as much of the white membrane as possible.

Cut out each full-length segment of grapefruit, using a sharp knife to separate the fruit from the membranes. Try not to break the segments. Put the grapefruit segments into the buttered baking dish and set aside.

Squeeze what remains of the grapefruit to extract the juice. There should be about ¾ cup. In a shallow baking dish combine the grapefruit juice with the olive oil, ginger, mustard, coriander and black pepper to taste. Whisk well.

Add the fish steaks to the baking dish and turn them to coat well with the marinade. Cover the dish and marinate the fish at room temperature for 30 minutes.

Preheat the broiler. If the broiler and oven are not part of the same unit (that is, if the oven does not get hot when the broiler is used), preheat the oven to 425ºF.

Uncover the baking dish and put it into the broiler 3 to 4 inches from the heat source. Put the baking dish with the grapefruit sections in it on a rack as low in the oven as possible. Broil the fish until it is lightly browned, firm to the touch, and flakes easily, about 4 minutes. Do not turn the fish.

Remove the fish from the broiler and the grapefruit sections from the oven. Arrange the fish steaks on a serving plate and sprinkle with the chopped scallions. Garnish the fish with the grapefruit segments and serve.

Marion Cunningham's Grilled Fish with Fresh Fruits

SERVES 6

SODIUM PER SERVING: 90 MG
CALORIES PER SERVING: 179

Marion Cunningham is the editor of *The Fannie Farmer Cookbook* and *The Fannie Farmer Baking Book*. She is highly regarded as a cooking teacher. The success of this recipe depends on fruit that is firm and slightly underripe so that the sharp acids balance the bland fish. Any firm, white-fleshed fish, such as scrod, cod, or flounder may be used.

vegetable oil
3 tablespoons unsalted butter
2 cups small cubes fresh pineapple
1 cup peeled, thinly sliced nectarine
1 tablespoon lemon zest
1½ pounds fresh fish fillets

Preheat the broiler to high. If cooking outdoors, the coals should be white. Brush the broiler pan or grill with vegetable oil.

Melt the butter in a skillet over low heat. Add the pineapple, nectarine and lemon zest. Cook, stirring frequently, until the fruit is thoroughly warmed. Remove the skillet from the heat.

Broil or grill the fish for 1½ to 2 minutes per side. Serve with the warm fruit.

Fish in Parchment

SERVES 4

SODIUM PER SERVING: 139 MG
CALORIES PER SERVING: 318

Cooking fish in parchment is a method of steaming fish in the oven instead of on top of the stove. Use parchment paper or heavy aluminum foil. Any fish steak or fillet can be cooked this way. Thin fillets or steaks require five minutes less.

4 8-ounce fish steaks
½ cup dry white wine
2 tablespoons unsalted butter
½ cup thinly sliced onion
1 carrot, peeled and julienned
½ cup thinly sliced scallion tops (green part)
½ cup finely chopped dill
2 teaspoons lime juice
freshly ground black pepper

Preheat the oven to 400°F.

Put the fish steaks into a shallow bowl. Pour the wine over them and marinate, turning occasionally, for 15 minutes.

Melt the butter in a small skillet over medium heat. Add the onion, carrot, and scallion tops. Cook, stirring occasionally, until the vegetables are soft, about 5 minutes. Remove the skillet from the heat.

Cut 4 pieces of kitchen parchment paper or heavy aluminum foil a little more than twice the size of each steak.

Pour 1 teaspoon of liquid from the skillet on the center of each piece of parchment or foil. Put a fish steak on top. Top each fish steak with one-quarter of the vegetable mixture and of the dill. Sprinkle each steak with ½ teaspoon of lime juice.

Fold the edges of the parchment or foil tightly together to make a leakproof seam. This is easiest to do if you fold the long seam first and then the ends. Put the fish packets on a baking sheet. Bake for 10 to 12 minutes.

To serve, place a packet on each plate. Open at the table with scissors or a sharp knife.

Baked Whole Fish

SERVES 4

SODIUM PER SERVING: 311 MG
CALORIES PER SERVING: 898

Striped bass, red snapper, bluefish, or mackerel are delicious prepared
this way. The vegetables are soft but still crisp, a nice contrast to the
tender fish. For an interesting variation, add ½ pint of fresh, small
oysters to the vegetable stuffing.

1 4-pound whole fish, cleaned, with head and tail
2 teaspoons olive oil
2 onions, thinly sliced
1 carrot, peeled and thinly sliced
1 green pepper, seeded and cut into the rings
3 tablespoons lemon juice
1 teaspoon chopped fresh thyme or ¼ teaspoon dried
1 teaspoon chopped fresh rosemary or ¼ teaspoon dried
½ cup chopped parsley
¼ cup chopped dill
freshly ground black pepper
2 tablespoons unsalted butter
½ teaspoon sweet paprika
1 cup red or white wine

Preheat the oven to 375ºF. With the olive oil, grease a roasting
pan large enough to hold the fish.

Arrange the onion, carrot, and green pepper in layers in the
cavity of the fish. Sprinkle with 1½ tablespoons of lemon
juice and the thyme, rosemary, parsley and dill. Add black
pepper to taste. Dot the stuffing with 1 tablespoon of butter.
Close the cavity with string or skewers.

Put the fish into the roasting pan. Sprinkle the remaining
lemon juice over the fish. Sprinkle with additional black
pepper to taste and the paprika. Dot the top of the fish with
the remaining butter. Pour the wine over the fish.

Bake the fish, basting often with the pan juices and adding
more butter if necessary, until the flesh is firm to the touch,
about 35 to 45 minutes.

Stuffed Fillets Baked in Lettuce Leaves

SERVES 4

SODIUM PER SERVING: 158 MG
CALORIES PER SERVING: 199

This is a quick and elegant way to prepare fish fillets. Any firm white fillet, such as sole, flounder, or red snapper, can be used. Serve with Ratatouille (see page 168) and rice tossed with lots of lemon juice and black pepper.

8 to 10 large romaine or *green leaf lettuce leaves*
2 ¾-pound fresh fish fillets, each about ¾-inch thick
1 cup finely chopped fresh parsley or chervil
1 cup chopped onion
1 carrot, peeled and grated
freshly ground black pepper to taste
½ cup white wine

Preheat the oven to 400°F.

Line the sides and bottom of a baking dish with the lettuce leaves. The leaves should hang over the edges of the dish.

Put 1 fillet into the dish. Cover it with the onion, carrot and parsley. Sprinkle with black pepper to taste. Top with the remaining fillet. Fold the ends of the lettuce leaves over the top fillet. Add the wine to the dish.

Cover the dish with aluminum foil and bake for 15 minutes. Remove the foil, fold back the lettuce leaves, and serve the fish immediately. Serve the steamed lettuce separately.

Poached Flounder with Saffron

SERVES 4

SODIUM PER SERVING: 187 MG
CALORIES PER SERVING: 266

Saffron adds a distinct aroma, pungency, and color to this dish. It is
expensive, but a little of it goes quite a long way. Serve with plain rice or
noodles to enjoy the extra sauce.

½ teaspoon dried whole-leaf thyme
½ teaspoon white peppercorns
10 parsley sprigs
1 cup water
1 cup white wine
2 bay leaves
1 medium-sized onion, quartered
4 8-ounce flounder fillets
¼ teaspoon hot red pepper flakes
8 ounces salt-free tomato purée
¼ teaspoon saffron
½ lemon, thinly sliced

Put the thyme, white peppercorns, and parsley into the center
of a 3-inch square of cheesecloth. Tie the cheesecloth closed
to form a bag, a *bouquet garni.*

Put the *bouquet garni,* water, white wine, bay leaves and
onion into a large skillet. Bring to a simmer over medium
heat and add the fish fillets. Cover the skillet and continue
to simmer until the fish is firm and flakes easily with a fork,
about 7 to 10 minutes. Remove the fish with a slotted
spoon, put it on a serving platter, and set aside in a warm
place. Remove the *bouquet garni,* bay leaves, and onion
and discard.

Add the tomato purée and the hot red pepper flakes
to the liquid in the skillet. Mix well and bring to the boil.
Continue to boil until the liquid is reduced by half, about
10 minutes. Add the saffron and half the lemon slices and
boil for 1 minute longer.

Spoon the sauce over the fish fillets. Garnish with the
remaining lemon slices and serve hot.

Grilled Monkfish Catalán

SERVES 4

SODIUM PER SERVING: 187 MG
CALORIES PER SERVING: 346

A versatile, firm-fleshed fish, monkfish is also called anglerfish or lotte. The fillets, taken from the tail, are usually thick and need a few extra minutes of cooking time. The flavor reminds many people of lobster. The onions and briefly cooked tomatoes in this recipe are characteristic of the cooking of Spain.

4 8-ounce monkfish fillets
olive oil
juice of ½ lemon

Tomato and Onion Sauce:

2 tablespoons olive oil
1 large garlic clove, minced
4 tablespoons chopped parsley
1 medium-sized onion, chopped
½ cup white wine
2 large ripe tomatoes, seeded and chopped
freshly ground black pepper

Preheat the broiler to high. Brush the fillets with olive oil and sprinkle them with the lemon juice.

Broil the fillets until they are firm to the touch and flake easily, about 7 minutes per side. When done, transfer the fillets to a serving platter and keep warm.

Heat the olive oil in a heavy skillet over medium heat. Add the garlic, parsley and onion. Cook, stirring frequently, until the onions are soft and golden brown. Add the white wine, lower the heat, and simmer for 5 minutes. Add the tomatoes and cook only until the tomato pieces are hot but still firm. Season to taste with black pepper.

Spoon the sauce over the monkfish fillets.
Serve immediately.

Broiled Fish Fillets with Green Sauce

SERVES 4

SODIUM PER SERVING: 175 MG
CALORIES PER SERVING: 462

Green sauce adds texture and flavor to any firm, white-fleshed fish
fillets. This sauce is also good served with baked or steamed fish, or
over poached chicken. It can be used as a salad dressing for tender
young greens. Serve this dish with steamed whole young vegetables,
such as baby carrots, young zucchini, or early green beans, and
a salad of cherry tomatoes and cucumber slices.

4 large fish fillets, each ½-inch thick
2 tablespoons melted unsalted butter

Green Sauce:

½ cup finely chopped fresh parsley leaves
½ cup finely chopped fresh dill
1 garlic clove, finely chopped
white of 1 hard-cooked egg, finely chopped
¼ teaspoon dry mustard
2 tablespoons lemon juice
¼ teaspoon coarsely ground black pepper
½ cup olive oil

Preheat the broiler.

First make the green sauce. In a small bowl combine the
parsley, dill, garlic, egg white, mustard, lemon juice, and
black pepper. Gradually add the oil, stirring constantly,
to make a thick sauce. Set aside.

Brush a broiling pan with half the butter. Put the fillets in
a single layer on the pan (do not use a rack) and drizzle the
remaining butter over them.

Broil the fillets 3 inches from the heat until they are firm,
white, and flake easily with a fork, about 5 minutes. Do not
turn the fillets.

Transfer the fillets to a serving platter and top each with a
small amount of the green sauce. Serve with the remaining
sauce on the side.

Marinated Seafood Salad

SERVES 4

SODIUM PER SERVING: 95 MG
CALORIES PER SERVING: 422

This seafood salad is simple and elegant, excellent for a first course. Any firm-fleshed fish steak can be used. Freeze the lime-scented broth and use it as a base for fish soup or for poaching.

2 bay leaves
2 garlic cloves
10 black peppercorns
½ lime, sliced
1½ pounds fish steaks
1 teaspoon pickling spices
¼ cup wine vinegar
½ cup olive oil
1 small onion, thinly sliced
½ lemon, thinly sliced

Bring enough water to cover the fish steaks to a slow boil in a large shallow skillet. Add the bay leaves, garlic, peppercorns, and lime. When the liquid returns to a simmer, add the fish steaks. Cover and simmer until the fish flakes easily away from the bone, about 10 minutes.

Remove the fish steaks from the skillet with a slotted spoon. Put the fish into a deep bowl. When it is cool enough to handle, remove the skin and bones. Break the fish into bite-sized pieces with a fork.

In a small bowl, combine the pickling spices, vinegar, and olive oil. Mix well and pour over the fish. Put the onion and lemon slices over the fish pieces. Baste with the vinegar and oil mixture that has accumulated in the bottom of the bowl. Refrigerate for at least 3 hours before serving, basting occasionally with liquid from the bottom of the bowl.
To serve, arrange the fish in a shallow bowl and garnish with the lemon and onion slices.

Escabèche

SERVES 4

SODIUM PER SERVING: 130 MG
CALORIES PER SERVING: 608

A traditional Spanish dish, escabèche can be served as a luncheon or light supper dish or as a first course. Because the fish is first cooked and then marinated, use a firm fish such as mackerel, bluefish, cod or tilefish so that the pieces will not fall apart.

1½ pounds fresh fish fillets, at least ½ inch thick
½ cup flour
freshly ground black pepper
½ cup olive oil
2 garlic cloves, crushed
⅛ teaspoon hot red pepper flakes
3 bay leaves
2 tablespoons vinegar
1 medium-sized sweet onion, thinly sliced
½ lemon, thinly sliced

Dust the fish fillets with the flour and black pepper to taste.

Heat the oil in a large, heavy skillet. When the oil is very hot, add the fish fillets and sauté on both sides until the fish is firm and flakes easily with a fork, about 5 minutes on each side. Remove the fish from the skillet, drain on paper towels and put into a serving bowl. Use a fork to break the fish into chunks.

Add the garlic, red pepper flakes, bay leaves and vinegar to the skillet. Bring to a boil and cook for 1 minute. Pour the marinade over the fish.

Marinate the fish in the refrigerator for at least 4 hours and preferably overnight, mixing occasionally.

Serve garnished with lemon and onion slices.

Sautéed Oysters

SERVES 4

SODIUM PER SERVING: 109 MG
CALORIES PER SERVING: 244

Oysters are the lowest in sodium of any shellfish. Shucked oysters are readily available at most supermarkets and fish stores. Use the smallest possible oysters. Cooked quickly, they remain tender and moist. Serve them with Tartar Sauce (see page 19) or lemon wedges and a dash of hot sauce.

2 pints freshly shucked oysters
3 tablespoons lemon juice
½ cup bread crumbs
freshly ground black pepper
½ cup chopped parsley
2 tablespoons vegetable oil
2 tablespoons unsalted butter
lemon wedges
Tartar Sauce (see page 19)

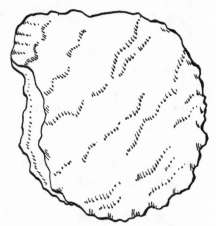

Preheat the oven to 180°F.

Drain the oysters well and sprinkle with the lemon juice.

On a flat plate, mix together the bread crumbs, black pepper to taste, and parsley. Coat the oysters on all sides with the mixture. Shake off any excess.

Heat the oil and butter together in a large, heavy skillet. When the mixture just begins to sizzle, add enough oysters to cover the bottom. Cook until the bottoms of the oysters are light brown, about 2 to 3 minutes. Turn with a spatula and cook until the other sides are lightly browned, about 2 to 3 minutes longer.

Remove the oysters from the skillet with a slotted spoon and drain on paper towels on a serving platter. Place the platter in the oven to keep warm while cooking the remaining oysters. Add additional butter and oil to the skillet if necessary.

Serve hot, garnished with the lemon wedges. Serve tartar sauce on the side.

Meat

Red meat, and beef in particular, is high in calories and also has more cholesterol and fat than most other sources of protein. However, we believe that many people go too far in their quest for a healthy diet when they completely eliminate red meat. If it is not restricted from your diet for medical reasons, there is no reason not to eat red meat occasionally in moderation. Many people who have reduced the amount of red meat in their diet find that they appreciate it more when they do have it.

Recipes for lamb, beef, veal, and pork dishes are included in this chapter. These meats require fairly assertive seasoning, but remember that the amounts of any of the spices and herbs given in the recipes can be adjusted to taste.

Roast Fillet of Beef with Green Peppercorns

SERVES 8 TO 10

SODIUM PER SERVING: 146 MG
CALORIES PER SERVING: 610

For a simple and elegant dinner party, serve this fillet of beef with Baked Potato Fans (see page 160), a quickly steamed fresh green vegetable, and a crisp salad.

1 tablespoon vegetable oil

4 tablespoons unsalted butter, softened

2 tablespoons green peppercorns, drained and rinsed

1 tablespoon coarsely ground black pepper

1 6-pound fillet of beef or beef tenderloin

1 bunch watercress

Preheat the oven to 425°F. Grease a rack that will fit into a shallow roasting pan with the vegetable oil.

In a small bowl using a wooden spoon, cream the butter and green peppercorns. Add the black pepper and mix well.

Coat the top and sides of the beef fillet with the peppercorn mixture. Put the meat on the rack in the roasting pan. Roast the meat for approximately 45 minutes, or until a meat thermometer reads 125°F., for medium-rare meat, and longer for more well-done meat.

Remove the fillet from the oven and let it rest for 10 minutes before slicing. Arrange the slices overlapping on a serving platter. Garnish with the watercress and serve.

Peppercorn Steak

SERVES 4
_____

SODIUM PER SERVING: 153 MG
CALORIES PER SERVING: 440

This rich, spicy steak dish goes well with Mushroom Melange
(see page 157) and wild rice. Use a combination of peppercorns, such as
Tellicherry, green, Madagascar, white and extra-hot Szechuan for additional
aroma and interest. If you like your peppercorns very coarse, fold them in
the corner of a clean kitchen towel and crush them with a heavy rolling
pin, mallet, or the side of a hammer.

4 shell steaks, 1½ to 2 inches thick, trimmed
3 tablespoons coarsely ground peppercorns
2 tablespoons unsalted butter
¼ cup chopped shallots
½ cup red wine
½ cup thinly sliced mushrooms
¼ cup chopped fresh parsley

Press the peppercorns firmly into both sides of each steak.

Melt the butter in a large, heavy skillet over high heat.
When the butter is very hot, add the steaks and quickly sear
them until they are brown on the bottom, about 1 minute.
Turn the steaks and sear the other side. Reduce the heat to
medium and continue cooking about 6 minutes longer on
each side for rare meat and 10 minutes on each side if you
prefer it more well done. Transfer the steaks to a serving
platter and keep warm.

Add the shallots to the skillet and sauté until they begin to
soften, about 3 minutes. Stir often, scraping the brown bits
from the side and bottom of the skillet. Add the wine and
mushrooms and continue to cook over high heat, stirring
frequently, until the sauce thickens, about 4 minutes.

Pour the sauce over the steaks. Garnish with parsley
and serve.

Barbecued Ribs

SERVES 4
_____
SODIUM PER SERVING: 124 MG
CALORIES PER SERVING: 823

Spareribs are delicious although a little messy to eat. Serve them at an informal meal with Potato Salad with White Wine Dressing (see page 60) and Coleslaw with Yogurt Dressing (see page 60). The ribs can be cooked over coals or in a broiler.

4 pounds pork spareribs, well trimmed
2 tablespoons vegetable oil
1¼ cups Barbecue Sauce (see page 30)

Put the ribs into a large pot. Add water to cover. Bring to the boil, then reduce the heat, and simmer for 40 minutes. Drain the ribs well.

In a small bowl, combine the oil and barbecue sauce. Blend well.

To cook the ribs on the grill place them on a grill over coals that have become white. Cook, turning often, for 10 to 12 minutes. Continue cooking for 12 to 15 minutes, brushing the sauce on the ribs and turning frequently.

To cook the ribs in the broiler, first preheat the broiler. Put the ribs on a rack in a broiler pan at least 6 inches from the heat. Cook as over a grill, brushing the sauce on the ribs after they have cooked for 12 minutes.

Turn frequently.

Whether the ribs are grilled or broiled, they are done when they are almost charred, bronze in color, and the fat has disappeared.

Serve with additional barbecue sauce on the side.

Pork Chops en Adobo

SERVES 4

SODIUM PER SERVING: 118 MG
CALORIES PER SERVING: 411

In the Philippines, *en adobo* refers to dishes cooked with a traditional combination of vinegar, garlic and black pepper. Serve these pork chops with rice and Apple Ginger Chutney (see page 32) and Paula's Quick Onion Relish (see page 26) on the side.

8 thinly cut, lean pork chops
4 garlic cloves, halved
3 bay leaves
6 tablespoons red wine vinegar
8 black peppercorns
1 cup boiling water

Put the pork chops, garlic, bay leaves, vinegar, peppercorns, and water into a large, heavy skillet. Let stand for 10 minutes.

Put the skillet on the stove and bring the liquid to a simmer over medium heat. Continue to cook until the liquid is gone and the fat on the chops begins to melt.

Remove the garlic and peppercorns from the skillet. Continue to cook until the bottoms of the pork chops are golden brown. Turn the pork chops and continue cooking until the other sides are browned.

Remove the pork chops from the skillet and serve hot.

Veal Stew with Lemon and Dill

SERVES 4

SODIUM PER SERVING: 172 MG
CALORIES PER SERVING: 523

The lemon and dill in this stew add flavor to the delicate meat. Good veal is almost white in color; veal that is red will be tough. This dish is easily halved if you are cooking for two. Serve it with rice, fettucini, or broad noodles.

1½ pounds stewing veal, cubed
½ cup flour for dredging
vegetable oil for browning
1 medium-sized onion, sliced
2 tablespoons lemon juice
1 cup water or Chicken Stock (see page 50)
1 cup white wine
½ pound mushrooms, sliced
2 cups shelled fresh peas
freshly ground black pepper
½ cup chopped fresh dill or 1 tablespoon dried
1 lemon, thinly sliced

Dredge the veal cubes in the flour.

In a deep, heavy skillet heat enough oil to cover the bottom. Add the onion and cook over medium heat, stirring frequently, until it is soft. Push the onion to the side of the skillet. Add the veal and cook, stirring constantly, until the meat loses it color. Do not crowd the skillet; if necessary, brown the veal in batches.

Sprinkle the veal with lemon juice. Add the water or chicken stock and the wine and mix well, stirring to scrape up all the brown bits from the side and bottom of the pan.

Reduce the heat, cover the skillet, and simmer gently for 45 minutes, or until the veal is tender. Stir occasionally and make sure there is sufficient liquid. If necessary, add more wine.

Add the mushrooms and peas. Cook for 15 minutes longer, or until the vegetables are tender but still crisp. Add black pepper to taste and mix well.

Spoon the stew into a serving dish. Sprinkle with the dill and garnish with the lemon slices.

Roast Shoulder of Veal with Chutney Apples

SERVES 6

SODIUM PER SERVING: 163 MG
CALORIES PER SERVING: 458

Serve this dish with rice or Orzo and Mushrooms (see page 116).

2½ pounds boned, rolled veal shoulder
2 garlic cloves, slivered
1 tablespoon salt-free Dijon-style mustard
1 tablespoon unflavored bread crumbs
freshly ground black pepper
1 tablespoon vegetable oil
4 apples, cored and sliced
juice of ½ lemon
4 tablespoons Apple Ginger Chutney (see page 32)
2 tablespoons unsalted butter

Preheat the oven to 350°F.

Using the point of a sharp knife, insert the garlic slivers into the rolled veal, distributing them evenly. Spread the mustard over the top of the veal.

In a small bowl mix the bread crumbs, pepper to taste and oil into a paste. Spread on top of the veal.

Roast the veal for 1 hour.

Remove the veal from the roasting pan and set aside. Arrange the apple slices on the bottom of the pan and sprinkle with the lemon juice. Spread the chutney over the apple slices. Dot them with the butter.

Put the veal on top of the apples and return the roasting pan to the oven. Cook for an additional 45 minutes, or until a meat thermometer reads 175°F. Remove the veal from the roasting pan and put it onto a cutting board. Let stand for 10 minutes before slicing.

Arrange the apple slices in the center of a serving platter. Arrange the veal slices around the apples and serve.

Charcoal Grilled Indian Lamb

SERVES 6

SODIUM PER SERVING: 191 MG
CALORIES PER SERVING: 500

The yogurt and spices add a tangy flavor to the lamb. Serve with Chutney Rice (see page 134) and Grilled Onions (see page 158).

1 6-pound leg of lamb, boned and butterflied
2 tablespoons olive oil
4 teaspoons ground cumin
2 teaspoons ground turmeric
1 cup unflavored low-fat yogurt
1 cup chopped onion
½ cup choped coriander
¼ cup finely chopped ginger
½ cup chopped fresh mint or ¼ cup dried

Trim as much fat as possible from the lamb. Divide the leg into 3 or 4 segments of approximately equal size for easy turning on the grill. Pierce the meat all over with a fork to help it absorb the marinade.

In a small bowl combine the oil, cumin and turmeric. Coat the lamb on all sides with the mixture.

In a large bowl combine the yogurt, onion, coriander, ginger and mint. Marinate the lamb in the mixture for 2 to 3 hours at room temperature, turning frequently.

Place the lamb on a grill 6 inches above white coals. Grill for 12 to 15 minutes on each side. Baste with the marinade before turning and again just before cooking is finished. Slice the lamb against the grain, sprinkle with the chopped fresh mint and serve.

Boned Leg of Lamb with Spinach Filling

SERVES 6 TO 8

SODIUM PER SERVING: 236 MG
CALORIES PER SERVING: 663

This dish is surprisingly easy to prepare. It needs only baked potatoes
and a delicate green salad to make an elegant main course.

1 6- to 7-pound leg of lamb, boned, flattened,
   and trimmed of all excess fat
juice of ½ lemon
3 garlic cloves, crushed
1 teaspoon dried rosemary
   or 1 tablespoon chopped fresh rosemary
¼ cup vegetable oil
2 tablespoons unsalted butter, softened
freshly ground black pepper
2 carrots, peeled and cut into thirds
2 large onions, quartered
1 cup water
2 cups red wine
1 tablespoon cornstarch

Spinach Filling:

1 pound fresh spinach
   or 2 10-ounce packages of thawed frozen, chopped spinach
1 small onion, finely chopped
2 eggs, beaten
¾ cup unflavored bread crumbs
⅓ cup slivered, toasted almonds
1 teaspoon dried rosemary
freshly ground black pepper

Preheat the oven to 350°F.

Sprinkle the lemon juice over the surface of the flattened
leg of lamb. Pierce gently with a fork all over on both sides.

Combine the garlic and rosemary with the oil to make
a paste. Brush the lamb with the paste.

Next, make the spinach filling. Carefully wash the spinach

to remove all grit. Remove any tough stems and blemished leaves. Put the spinach into a large pot and cook over medium heat, stirring constantly until it is bright green and wilted. Do not add any water; the spinach will cook in the water that clings to the leaves from the washing. Squeeze the cooked spinach dry, then chop it. If thawed frozen spinach is being used, squeeze it dry.

Put the spinach into a large bowl and add the onion, beaten eggs, bread crumbs, almonds, rosemary, and black pepper. Mix well.

Put the spinach filling in the center of the lamb. Close the leg and tie it with butcher's string. Put the lamb in a roasting pan, seam-side down. Make a line of butter pats on the top of the lamb. Sprinkle with black pepper.

Surround the roast with the carrots and onions. Add the water and 1 cup red wine to the roasting pan. Roast for 2 hours, basting the lamb frequently and turning the vegetables so they brown evenly. When the roast is done, remove it and the vegetables from the roasting pan and put them on a platter. Keep warm. Let the lamb rest for at least 15 minutes before removing the string and slicing it.

Skim off and discard the excess fat from the pan juices. Put the roasting pan over medium heat. Using a wooden spoon, scrape all the meat particles and brown bits from the sides and bottom of the roasting pan. Add the remaining cup of red wine.

Remove 4 tablespoons of the pan juices and put them into a small bowl. Add the cornstarch and stir to dissolve. Return the mixture to the pan. Raise the heat and boil the sauce, stirring frequently, until it is reduced by half.

Arrange the sliced lamb and the vegetables on a serving platter and serve with the sauce.

Lamb and Roast Pepper Salad

SERVES 4

SODIUM PER SERVING: 100 MG
CALORIES PER SERVING: 510

This main dish salad is an excellent way to use leftover lamb. The salad
can be made well in advance if it is kept covered in the refrigerator.

2 large sweet red peppers
2 garlic cloves, minced
freshly ground black pepper
2 teaspoons fresh sweet marjoram leaves
  or 2 teaspoons parsley leaves
5 teaspoons wine vinegar
5 teaspoons lemon juice
8 tablespoons olive oil
3 to 4 cups cold roast lamb, thickly julienned
1 cup sliced sweet onion

Put the peppers on a baking sheet under the broiler.
Cook them, turning occasionally, until all sides of the
peppers are black. Remove them from the broiler and place
them in a paper bag. Close the bag and wait until the
peppers are cool enough to handle, about 10 minutes.
Peel off the skins. Cut the peppers into halves and remove the
stems and seeds. Cut the peppers into strips, rinse them if
necessary, and put them into a bowl.

In a small bowl, mash the garlic with black pepper to taste.
Add the marjoram or parsley and crush slightly with the
back of a spoon. Add the vinegar and lemon juice. Slowly
whisk in the olive oil.

To make the salad, put the lamb, onions and peppers into a
serving bowl. Add the vinaigrette and toss well. Garnish with
some herb sprigs and serve at room temperature.

Osso Buco

SERVES 4

SODIUM PER SERVING: 315 MG
CALORIES PER SERVING: 793

This classic Italian dish is made with veal shanks. It needs slow cooking
and some attention from the cook. The delicious results are worth the
effort. Veal shanks vary widely in size. Often, but not always, one piece
per serving is ample. It is best to judge the amount to purchase while at
the butcher shop. Osso buco is a very good company dish. It is traditionally garnished with gremolata, a mixture of lemon rind, garlic, and parsley,
and served with Italian short-grain rice cooked in chicken broth. A crusty
loaf of Italian bread and a bottle of robust red wine complete the meal.

2½ to 3 pounds thickly sliced veal shanks
¾ cup flour
freshly ground black pepper
6 tablespoons olive oil
1 cup coarsely chopped onions
3 large carrots, peeled and chopped
3 garlic cloves, chopped
1 cup dry red wine
2 cups Chicken Stock (see page 50) or salt-free beef stock
1 28-ounce can salt-free whole tomatoes, drained and chopped
1 teaspoon dried oregano
3 bay leaves

Gremolata:
2 tablespoons grated lemon rind
1 tablespoon minced garlic
3 tablespoons finely chopped parsley

Wipe the veal shanks with a damp paper towel.
Put the flour on a large flat plate. Add black pepper to taste
and mix well. Dredge the veal shanks in the flour mixture.
Shake off any excess.

Heat the olive oil in a large heavy skillet. When the oil is hot,
add the veal shanks and brown well on each side. Do not
crowd the shanks as they brown; if necessary, brown them in
batches. When the shanks are browned, remove them from
the skillet and put them on a platter.

Add the onions, carrots, and garlic to the skillet.
Cook, stirring frequently, until the vegetables are soft,
about 5 to 7 minutes. Remove the vegetables from the
skillet with a slotted spoon and put them into a large
heavy pot with a tightly fitting lid. Add the veal shanks to
the pot and set aside.

Pour off the oil from the skillet and return it to the heat.
Add the wine and bring to a rapid boil. Continue to cook,
scraping the sides and bottom of the skillet with a wooden
spoon to loosen the brown bits clinging to them, until the
sauce starts to thicken, about 2 to 3 minutes.

Pour the sauce from the skillet into the pot with the vegetables and veal shanks. Add the stock, tomatoes, oregano,
and bay leaves to the pot. Bring the mixture to a boil, then
lower the heat. Cover the pot and simmer until the meat is
very tender, about 1½ to 2 hours. Baste often. If more liquid
is needed, add additional stock.

Prepare the gremolata as the veal shanks cook.
Put the lemon rind, garlic, and parsley into a small bowl
and mix well. Gremolata is not cooked.

Remove the veal shanks from the pot and put them on
a serving platter. Keep warm.

Remove the bay leaves from the pot and discard. Skim off
as much fat as possible from the liquid in the pot. Strain the
liquid and vegetables through a fine sieve back into the pot.
Using the back of a spoon, push the vegetables through the
sieve. Alternatively, put the liquid and vegetables into the
container of a food processor or blender, process until
smooth, and return to the pot.

Bring the sauce to the boil and taste to correct the seasonings. Add a pinch of sugar if the tomatoes are acid-tasting.

To serve, spoon the sauce over the veal shanks and sprinkle
with the gremolata. Serve immediately.

Poultry

Poultry dishes are versatile. A wide range of cooking techniques, including frying, poaching and roasting, can be used, and, as the recipes in this chapter prove, poultry is particularly well complemented by herbs, spices, and other flavorings. In addition to being easy to cook without salt, poultry is low in calories, fats, and cholesterol.

Today, as the result of mass-production techniques, most of the poultry, particularly the chickens, that are readily available are uniform in size and lacking in flavor. The bright yellow of their skins is the result of chemical additives to their feed. It is still possible, however, to buy chickens that have not been raised on an assembly line. These chickens, sometimes called free-range chickens, are bred in a less confined environment and are given feed that does not contain as many chemicals. Their naturally good flavor and texture make them worth the higher price. Always try to buy fresh chicken, rather than frozen, and always cook it as soon as possible.

In most markets it is difficult to find a fresh turkey, much less a free-range turkey. If you must buy a frozen turkey, avoid the self-basting kind; these are injected with vegetable oil and may also contain added salt.

Breast of Chicken with Mushrooms

SERVES 4

SODIUM PER SERVING: 90 MG
CALORIES PER SERVING: 259

Serve this light and tasty dish with rice or broad noodles, or try it with Barley Casserole with Dried Mushrooms (see page 132). A green salad, a crusty loaf of French bread, and fresh fruit will complete the meal.

2 teaspoons vegetable oil
½ pound mushrooms, sliced
1 onion, sliced
4 garlic cloves, slivered
2 whole chicken breasts, split and skinned
3 tablespoons Vinaigrette (see page 20)
2 tablespoons red wine
2 teaspoons fresh tarragon or ½ teaspoon dried

Heat the oil in a heavy skillet over medium heat. Add the mushrooms, onions, and garlic and cook, stirring frequently, until the mushrooms begin to give up liquid, about 10 minutes.

Arrange the chicken breasts on top of the mushroom mixture. Spoon the vinaigrette over the chicken. Add the red wine and tarragon. Cover and cook over moderate heat for 15 minutes, basting frequently. Remove the cover and cook for 10 minutes longer, or until the chicken is firm and white all the way through.

Transfer the chicken breasts to a serving platter, spoon the mushroom mixture over them, and serve immediately.

Deviled Chicken

SERVES 4

SODIUM PER SERVING: 221 MG
CALORIES PER SERVING: 310

Chicken legs and thighs, even when skinned, are less likely to dry out when broiled than other parts of the bird. This dish is low in fat but still deliciously juicy.

6 tablespoons salt-free Dijon-style mustard
3 tablespoons vegetable oil
½ cup unflavored bread crumbs
4 chicken legs, skinned
4 chicken thighs, skinned

In a small bowl combine the mustard, 2 tablespoons of oil, and the bread crumbs.

Put the chicken pieces in a shallow dish. Brush the pieces on all sides with the mustard mixture. Let stand at room temperature for at least 30 minutes, turning occasionally. Reserve the mixture left in the dish.

Preheat the broiler for 15 minutes.

Put the coated chicken pieces, skin-side down, on a broiler pan or oiled rack. Broil until the pieces begin to brown, about 5 to 6 minutes. Turn the pieces and baste with the pan drippings. Broil for 5 minutes longer. Remove from the broiler.

Baste the chicken with the pan drippings, any leftover mustard mixture, and the remaining tablespoon of oil. Return the chicken to the broiler and cook until golden brown, about 2 to 3 minutes longer.

Serve immediately with additional mustard on the side.

Felipe Rojas-Lombardi's Chicken a la Gallega

SERVES 6

SODIUM PER SERVING: 92 MG
CALORIES PER SERVING: 279

Felipe Rojas-Lombardi is chef and owner of The Ballroom,
a popular restaurant and *tapas* bar in New York City. *Tapas* are
Spanish hôrs d'oeuvres. This recipe can be served as a *tapa*
for 12 or as a main course for 6.

3 large whole chicken breasts
2 teaspoons paprika
1 tablespoon olive oil
5 garlic cloves
1 bay leaf
⅛ teaspoon cayenne pepper
1 tablespoon flour
½ cup Chicken Stock (see page 50)

Preheat the oven to 450°F.

Put the chicken breasts, skin-side up, on a rack in
a roasting pan. Sprinkle the breasts with ½ teaspoon
of the paprika. Roast the breasts until golden brown,
about 25 minutes.

Remove the roasting pan from the oven and let the
chicken cool. When the breasts are cool enough to handle,
bone them and set aside.

Heat the olive oil in a small skillet over medium heat.
Add the garlic and the bay leaf. Sauté until the garlic is
brown, then add the remaining paprika, the cayenne
pepper and the flour. Mix well and gradually add the
chicken stock. Bring the mixture to a boil, stirring gently
and constantly to prevent lumps. Reduce the heat to low
and continue to cook, stirring constantly, until the sauce
is thickened.

Halve the chicken breasts and cut each half diagonally
into 3 pieces, preserving the shape of the breast. Arrange
the breasts on a serving platter and pour the hot sauce
over them. Serve at once.

Herb-Grilled Chicken with Mustard

SERVES 4

SODIUM PER SERVING: 157 MG
CALORIES PER SERVING: 349

This highly seasoned chicken dish is delicious cooked over coals or in the broiler. Reduce the amounts of garlic, rosemary and mustard by half for a milder flavor.

1 2½-pound chicken, cut into serving pieces
4 tablespoons vegetable oil
2 garlic cloves, crushed
½ teaspoon dried rosemary
freshly ground black pepper
3 tablespoons lemon juice
3 tablespoons salt-free Dijon-style mustard

Put the chicken pieces into a shallow dish.

Heat the oil in a small skillet over medium heat. Add the garlic, rosemary, and black pepper to taste. Cook until the garlic is lightly browned. Add 2 tablespoons of the lemon juice and stir well.

Pour the marinade over the chicken pieces. Turn the pieces to coat them well. Let the pieces marinate for 2 hours at room temperature, turning occasionally.

In a small bowl, combine the remaining lemon juice and the mustard. Mix well.

Preheat the broiler or prepare white coals for grilling.

Brush a rack in a broiler pan or the grill with oil. Put the chicken on the rack or grill and cook, turning frequently and basting often with the remaining marinade, until tender, about 25 to 30 minutes. Baste with the lemon juice and mustard mixture for the last few minutes of cooking. Serve immediately with additional mustard on the side.

Vinegar Sautéed Chicken

SERVES 4

SODIUM PER SERVING: 181 MG
CALORIES PER SERVING: 377

The liberal use of vinegar in this recipe adds an interesting flavor to a basically simple dish. Serve it with rice, Sesame Green Beans (see page 144), and Fennel Salad (see page 64).

1 3-pound chicken, cut into serving pieces
freshly ground black pepper
2 tablespoons unsalted butter
1 tablespoon olive oil
1 cup chopped onion
3 garlic cloves, chopped
½ cup red wine vinegar
1 cup water or Chicken Stock (see page 50)
2 tablespoons chopped fresh
   or ½ teaspoon dried tarragon or thyme

Season the chicken pieces with black pepper to taste.

Melt the butter and oil together in a large skillet over medium heat. Add the chicken pieces, skin-side down, and saute until golden brown, about 6 minutes. Turn the pieces and sauté until the other sides are golden brown, about 6 minutes longer.

Remove the chicken pieces from the skillet and set aside. Pour off all but 1 tablespoon of fat from the skillet. Return the skillet to the heat and add the onions and garlic. Sauté, stirring frequently, for about 7 minutes. Add the vinegar to the skillet and cook, stirring frequently, for 2 minutes longer. Add the water or chicken stock and the tarragon or thyme. Stir well. Bring the mixture to a boil, then reduce the heat.

Return the chicken pieces to the skillet. Cover the skillet and cook the chicken pieces, turning them twice, until they are tender, about 12 minutes. Serve immediately.

Chicken and Dumplings

SERVES 4

SODIUM PER SERVING: 199 MG
CALORIES PER SERVING: 672

A complete and satisfying one-dish meal, this dish can be served from a platter, with cups of broth on the side, or in deep individual soup bowls. Either way, be sure it is hot and steaming when brought to the table. Serve a first course of Eggplant Salad (see page 35) or Mushroom Pâté (see page 39) and end the meal with a fruit compote.

3 dill sprigs
3 parsley sprigs
1 2½- to 3-pound frying chicken, cut into serving pieces
chicken giblets (except the liver)
2 medium-sized carrots, cut into thick rounds
2 medium-sized onions, quartered
2 parsnips, cut into thick rounds
½ teaspoon white pepper
2 tablespoons chopped fresh dill or parsley

Dumplings:

1½ cups flour
1 egg, well beaten
⅓ cup plus 2 tablespoons finely chopped parsley
½ cup low-fat milk
1 teaspoon white pepper

Tie the parsley and dill sprigs together with butcher's string or white thread. Put the chicken, giblets, carrots, onions, parsnips, pepper, chopped dill or parsley, and parsley and dill sprigs into a large stock pot. Add enough water to cover. Bring to a boil, then reduce the heat and simmer for 45 to 60 minutes, or until the chicken is tender. Use a large spoon to skim off the fat and foam as it rises to the surface.

While the chicken cooks, begin preparing the dumplings. Put the flour into a large mixing bowl.

In another bowl, stir together the egg, ⅓ cup chopped parsley, milk, and pepper. Add to the flour and mix well. Refrigerate the batter until ready to use.

When the chicken is done, remove and discard the parsley and dill sprigs. With a slotted spoon, transfer the chicken pieces, giblets, and vegetables to a deep, ovenproof serving bowl or platter. Place in a very low oven to keep warm.

Bring the broth remaining in the pot to a slow boil. Drop the dumpling batter by rounded teaspoons into the broth. Cover the pot tightly and simmer for 15 minutes — do not lift the lid during this time.

Remove the dumplings with a slotted spoon and add them to the chicken and vegetables. Spoon some broth over the dish and garnish with the remaining 2 tablespoons of chopped parsley. Serve immediately.

Herbed Paillards of Chicken

SERVES 4

SODIUM PER SERVING: 78 MG
CALORIES PER SERVING: 253

Paillards are thin slices of poultry or meat that have been pounded to make them even thinner, no more than ¼-inch thick. They are cooked very rapidly in a heavy, ridged iron skillet or over coals. Boneless chicken breasts make excellent paillards, as does veal and turkey breast. Although this recipe calls for chicken paillards, it can be made with veal or turkey. The total amount of poultry or meat should be about 1½ pounds. Any combination of fresh and dried herbs, such as parsley, coriander, chives, thyme, and marjoram can be used.

2 whole chicken breasts, skinned and boned
3 tablespoons finely chopped fresh parsley or other fresh
*   herbs or 1 tablespoon dried parsley or other dried herbs*
¼ cup vegetable oil
freshly ground black pepper to taste
lemon wedges for garnish

Cut the chicken breasts into thin slices about ⅓-inch thick. Put each slice between two pieces of waxed paper or plastic wrap. Using a mallet or the flat side of a cleaver or large knife, gently pound the slices until they are flattened to paillards that are about ¼-inch thick. Remove the plastic wrap.

Combine the herbs and oil in a large, shallow dish. Add the paillards, turning them to coat them with the oil and herbs. Cover the dish and refrigerate for at least 2 hours.

Remove the dish from the refrigerator and allow the paillards to return to room temperature before cooking them.

Brush the skillet with oil and heat it over high heat. If cooking over coals, brush the grill with oil and cook over white coals. Add the paillards to the skillet or grill, in batches if necessary, and cook very briefly, about 1 to 2 minutes per side.

Garnish with lemon wedges and serve immediately.

Parsley-Stuffed Chicken Breasts

SERVES 4

SODIUM PER SERVING: 188 MG
CALORIES PER SERVING: 323

This dish may be made with fish fillets instead of chicken breasts. Put the filling between two fillets and cook for the same time as the chicken.

4 whole small chicken breasts, boned and skinned
2 cups coarsely chopped fresh parsley
1 large carrot, peeled and grated
½ medium-sized onion, chopped
2 garlic cloves, chopped
½ teaspoon dried whole-leaf thyme
    or 1 tablespoon chopped fresh thyme
1½ tablespoons salt-free Dijon-style mustard
freshly ground black pepper
½ cup white wine

Put the chicken breasts between sheets of waxed paper or plastic wrap on a cutting board. Using a mallet or the flat side of a cleaver or large knife, lightly flatten the breasts until they are about ½-inch thick. Set aside.

Put the parsley, carrots, onion, and garlic into a saucepan. Add 1 tablespoon water. Cover the saucepan and cook over medium heat, stirring occasionally, until the vegetables are soft.

Finely chop the cooked vegetables. Blend in the thyme, mustard, and pepper to taste. Divide the stuffing into 4 equal portions. Spread each portion on half a chicken breast and cover with the other half. Press firmly.

Put the chicken breasts into a serving bowl that will fit into a large pot or steamer. Pour the wine over the chicken. Invert a bowl that is about 4 inches deep and small enough to fit into the pot and place it in the bottom of the pot. Fill the pot with water to a depth of 2 inches. Place the bowl with the chicken on the inverted bowl (the water should not touch the serving bowl), cover the pot, and cook over medium heat for 12 to 15 minutes, or until the chicken is tender. The water should boil for the entire time. (A cooking rack that will hold the serving dish above the water may be used instead of an inverted bowl.)

Serve with the pan juices spooned over each breast.

Chicken Salad with Yams

SERVES 4

SODIUM PER SERVING: 42 MG
CALORIES PER SERVING: 186

This main-dish salad has a delightful variety of textures. Serve it on a bed of greens for lunch or supper. It's a good way to use leftover chicken or turkey, and the dressing is light and low in calories.

2 cups Quick Poaching Stock (see page 22)
2 large whole chicken breasts, skinned and boned
2 medium-sized yams, cooked, peeled, halved,
    and cut into ½-inch slices
1 8-ounce can water chestnuts, drained and sliced
2 small whole scallions, thinly sliced
½ cup unflavored low-fat yogurt
2 tablespoons Apple Ginger Chutney (see page 32)
1 teaspoon salt-free Dijon-style mustard
1 tablespoon red wine vinegar

In a deep skillet, bring the stock to a simmer.
Add the chicken breasts, cover the skillet, and simmer until the chicken is firm and white, about 15 to 18 minutes.

Remove the chicken breasts with a slotted spoon and put them into a small bowl. Continue to simmer the poaching liquid until it is reduced by half, about 10 minutes longer.

When the chicken is cool enough to handle, cut the breasts into 1-inch chunks and put them into a salad bowl. Add the yams, water chestnuts, and scallions to the bowl.

In a small bowl, combine ½ cup of the reduced poaching liquid, the yogurt, chutney, mustard, and vinegar. Mix well and pour over the ingredients in the salad bowl. Mix gently and serve.

Giblet Basting Broth

MAKES 3

SODIUM PER RECIPE: LESS THAN 0.5 MG
CALORIES PER RECIPE: LESS THAN 5

Prepare this broth before you begin roasting the turkey so that the giblets can then be used for the stuffing or gravy. If any broth remains after the turkey is cooked, discard the vegetables, strain the broth through a fine sieve and refrigerate or freeze it for future use as a base for soup.

giblets of 1 turkey (neck, heart, gizzard, liver, and wing tips)
2 carrots, peeled
1 onion
4 cups water

Put the giblets, carrots, and onion into a saucepan and add the water. Bring to a slow boil and cook until no pink shows in the liver and it is cooked through. Remove the liver and reserve it for another use.

Continue to boil the broth, skimming often to remove the foam and fat that rise to the top. When the giblets are soft, remove them from the broth and reserve them for another use. Reduce the heat to very low. Continue to simmer the broth while it is used to baste the turkey.

Holiday Roast Turkey

SERVES 12

SODIUM PER SERVING: 276 MG
CALORIES PER SERVING: 528

Roast turkey is a favorite in our house. It is especially favored as a main course at holiday times, when the number of guests has a tendency to expand at the last moment. When choosing a turkey, a generous estimate is one pound of uncooked turkey per expected guest. This allows for delicious leftover turkey sandwiches, midnight snacks, and general nibbling.

There are no hard and fast rules for seasoning a turkey. Use such fresh herbs as rosemary, thyme, sage, and oregano generously. Stuffing, too, follows no rules. Add or subtract ingredients according to your taste. Try adding walnuts, pecans, or pine nuts, and experiment with different kinds of mushrooms — fresh, woodland, or dried.

Ideally, a roast turkey is golden on the outside with tender, juicy meat. It should never be overcooked. Estimate about 15 minutes to the pound for an unstuffed turkey and 20 minutes to the pound for one that is stuffed. The bird is done when a meat thermometer reads 190ºF., the leg joints move easily, and no pink shows between the joints.

1 12- to 14-pound turkey, fresh or thawed
1 lemon, halved
1 apple, cored and halved
2 onions, halved
2 garlic cloves, minced
2 tablespoons salt-free Dijon-style mustard
4 tablespoons corn oil
4 teaspoons paprika
2 teaspoons black pepper
2 tablespoons flour
1½ teaspoons dried sage or crushed rosemary leaves
Giblet Basting Broth (see opposite page)

Preheat the oven to 375ºF.

Rub the cavity of the turkey with the lemon halves.
Put the apple and onion halves in the cavity.

In a small bowl, combine the garlic, mustard, oil, paprika, black pepper, flour, and sage or rosemary. Blend well.
Spread the mixture over the turkey with a pastry brush.

Place the turkey, breast-side down, in a roasting pan. Roast it for 30 minutes at 375ºF., then reduce the heat to 325ºF. and continue roasting for another 2½ to 3 hours, or until a meat thermometer inserted between the thigh and the body of the turkey reads 190°F. Turn the turkey breast-side up when it is golden brown, after about 2 hours. Baste frequently with the pan juices and the giblet basting broth.

Remove the turkey from the oven when done. Let stand for at least 15 minutes before carving.

Old-Fashioned Bread Stuffing

SERVES 12 TO 14

SODIUM PER SERVING: 66 MG
CALORIES PER SERVING: 90

We prefer to make stuffing without giblets in a separate dish so that vegetarian guests can enjoy it too. If you prefer the traditional inside-the-bird approach, put the stuffing into the turkey only when you are ready to put the bird into the oven, not before. Stuffing can also be made in advance and reheated. Cover the baking dish with aluminum foil and cook it for only 45 minutes. Reheat it for 15 minutes in the oven before serving.

¼ cup vegetable oil
2 medium-sized onions, diced
2 medium-sized carrots, peeled and diced
1 green pepper, seeded and diced
2 tablespoons chopped parsley
4 cups toasted bread, soaked in water and squeezed dry
cooked giblets of 1 turkey, coarsely chopped (optional)
2 eggs, well beaten
1 teaspoon dried sage
coarsely ground black pepper

Preheat the oven to 375°F.

Heat the oil in a skillet. Add the onions, carrots, green pepper, and parsley. Cook over medium heat until the vegetables are soft. Remove the vegetables from the skillet with a slotted spoon and put them into a deep mixing bowl. Reserve the oil.

Add the bread and giblets (if you are using them) to the vegetables in the mixing bowl. Mix well. Add the eggs, sage, and black pepper. Mix well.

Spread the stuffing in a shallow baking dish. Drizzle the oil from the skillet over the stuffing. Bake for 1 hour.

Turkey Gravy

MAKES 2½ CUPS

SODIUM PER SERVING (2 tablespoons): 1 MG
CALORIES PER SERVING: 10

Make the gravy while the turkey is resting before being carved.

½ cup dry red wine
2 cups turkey or chicken broth
cooked giblets of 1 turkey, coarsely chopped (optional)
2 tablespoons cornstarch
freshly ground black pepper

Pour off as much fat as possible from the roasting pan after the turkey has been removed. Put the pan over medium heat and add the wine. Scrape the sides and bottom of the pan with a wooden spoon to loosen the brown particles clinging to them. Stir the particles into the wine. Bring the mixture to a boil. Add the broth and stir well. Continue to boil until the mixture begins to thicken. Add the giblets (if you are using them) and continue to cook.

As the broth and wine mixture cooks, remove 5 tablespoons of the liquid and put them into a small bowl or cup.
Add the cornstarch and mix well until the liquid is smooth and there are no lumps. Pour the cornstarch mixture back into the roasting pan and stir well. Cook until the alcohol in the wine has evaporated, about 5 minutes longer. Add black pepper to taste and stir well.

Pour the gravy into a sauceboat. Serve hot with the turkey.

Glazed Turkey Breast

SERVES 8 TO 12

SODIUM PER SERVING: 146 MG
CALORIES PER SERVING: 424

This is a terrific buffet dish served warm or at room temperature.
The chutney glaze gives the turkey breast a lovely color and flavor.
The leftovers are great in sandwiches and salads. A large roasting
chicken (about 4½ pounds) may be substituted for the turkey breast;
roast the chicken for 70 to 80 minutes.

1 6-pound turkey breast, fresh or frozen and thawed
½ lemon
2 tablespoons melted unsalted butter
½ cup Apple Ginger Chutney (see page 32)
2 garlic cloves, minced (optional)

Preheat the oven to 375°F.

Place the turkey breast on a rack in a roasting pan. Rub the skin with the lemon half and brush with the melted butter.

In a small bowl, combine the chutney and garlic. Brush the mixture over the turkey.

Roast, basting frequently with the remaining chutney and the pan juices, for 80 to 90 minutes, or until a meat thermometer inserted into the center of the breast reads 190°F. There should be no pink around the bone.

Cornish Hens with Apricots

SERVES 4
_____

SODIUM PER SERVING: 133 MG
CALORIES PER SERVING: 559

This recipe calls for only half a Cornish hen per serving, an adequate portion for most diners. For more generous servings, allow a whole hen per person and double the remaining ingredients. Cornish hens can get dry easily; remember to baste them often with the sauce as they cook. Serve this dish with plain rice or delicate noodles.

2 Cornish game hens, with giblets
1 carrot, peeled
1 small onion, peeled
1 bay leaf
6 black peppercorns
1½ cups water or Chicken Stock (see page 50)
12 large dried apricots
2 tablespoons unsalted butter
1 cup white wine

Split the hens in half. Wash and pat them dry.

Put the giblets (including the liver) in a small saucepan. Add the carrot, onion, bay leaf, peppercorns and water.

Simmer over medium heat until the giblets are soft, about 25 minutes. With a spoon, skim off the foam and fat that rises to the surface as the giblets cook.

Put the dried apricots into a small bowl and add enough warm water to cover them. Set aside to soak for at least 30 minutes.

Strain the broth in the saucepan into a bowl through a sieve lined with cheesecloth. Set the broth aside. Remove the giblets from the sieve and set aside. Discard the carrot, onion, bay leaf, peppercorns, and any other solids that remain in the cheesecloth.

Coarsely chop the giblets and set aside.

Melt the butter in a large, nonstick skillet over medium heat. Add the hen halves, skin-side down, and cook until they are lightly browned, about 10 minutes. Turn the hens and brown them on the other side. Add more butter to the skillet if necessary.

Preheat the oven to 350°F.

Remove the hens from the skillet and put them into a baking dish. Sprinkle the hens with the chopped giblets.

Add the wine to the skillet. With a wooden spoon, stir and scrape the sides and bottom of the skillet to loosen the brown bits clinging to them. Bring the wine to a boil and cook until it is reduced by half. Add the reserved broth. Simmer the mixture for 1 minute.

Pour the wine and broth mixture over the hens. Drain the apricots and add them to the baking dish.
Bake, basting often with the sauce, until the hens are tender, about 30 minutes. Serve immediately.

Cornish Hens with Rice and Mushroom Stuffing

SERVES 4

SODIUM PER SERVING: 154 MG
CALORIES PER SERVING: 652

Cornish hens are more tender and meatier than most small birds. They are available fresh at most supermarkets. Serve this dish with Yam, Turnip, and Apple Puree (see page 163).

1 tablespoon vegetable oil
2 tablespoons chopped parsley (no stems)
1 small onion, thinly sliced
2 garlic cloves, minced
giblets of 2 Cornish hens (livers, hearts and gizzards), chopped
½ pound mushrooms, stems removed and caps thinly sliced
1 cup cooked rice
¼ teaspoon dried whole-leaf thyme
freshly ground black pepper
2 Cornish game hens
2 tablespoons unsalted butter, softened
½ teaspoon paprika
1 cup dry red or white wine

Preheat the oven to 400°F.

Heat the olive oil in a nonstick skillet over medium heat. Add the parsley, onion, garlic and giblets. Cook, stirring frequently with a wooden spoon, until the onion and giblets are soft. Add the mushrooms and continue to cook until the mushrooms begin to soften and give up their liquid. Add the rice and cook until it is heated through. Add the thyme and black pepper to taste.

Fill the cavities of the hens with the stuffing. Close the cavities with skewers. Put the hens, breast-side down, on a rack in a roasting pan. Spread 1 tablespoon of the butter on each hen and sprinkle each with ¼ teaspoon of paprika and black pepper to taste.

Roast the hens for 20 minutes. Turn the hens breast-side up and roast until the juices run clear, about 20 minutes longer. Remove the hens from the pan and put them on a carving board. Using a sharp knife or poultry shears, cut the hens in half. Carefully tuck the stuffing under each portion. Put the hen halves on a serving platter and keep warm.

Remove the rack from the roasting pan and put the pan on the stove over medium heat. Add the wine to the pan. With a wooden spoon, stir and scrape the bottom and sides of the pan to loosen any brown bits clinging to them. Raise the heat and bring the liquid to a slow boil. Cook, stirring frequently, until the liquid is reduced by half. Season the sauce to taste with black pepper, pour it over the hens, and serve.

Pasta, Grains, and Bread

Pastas, grains, and breads are high in nourishing carbohydrates and low in calories. Besides being good for you, they are delicious and filling. The recipes in this chapter borrow ideas from many international cuisines.

Most pasta, whether domestic or imported, fresh or dried, is made from semolina flour, a coarsely ground form of durum wheat. Pasta can also be made from whole wheat flour, buckwheat flour (used in many Japanese noodle dishes), and even from a flour made from Jerusalem artichokes. Before trying a new type of pasta, however, carefully read the ingredients list on the label — some have salt added.

Pasta comes in many sizes and shapes. We have kept to the readily available types, such as linguini and spaghetti, but in almost every recipe any pasta shape will work equally well.

Most pasta recipes routinely recommend cooking the pasta in a large pot of boiling salted water. They are right about the large pot and the boiling water, but the pasta will be just as good without the salt. Use at least five or more quarts of rapidly boiling water per pound of pasta. Add all the pasta to the pot at once and stir well. If the pasta cooks in lots of rapidly boiling water and is stirred frequently, the individual pieces won't stick together. Cook the pasta until it is *al dente*. In Italian, this means literally "to the tooth." In cooking, it means slightly resistant to the bite — never soft or mushy. A good general rule is to cook dried pasta for about 6 to 9 minutes, tasting often to avoid overcooking. Fresh pasta cooks much more quickly than dried; dried whole wheat pasta takes a little longer. When the pasta is done, drain it well in a colander so that water clinging to the pasta won't dilute the sauce.

In Western societies, the most common grain is wheat, the basis for most bread and pasta. In many other societies, wheat is less common, at least in these forms, and other grains are popular. Rice (white and brown), barley, bulghur wheat, and couscous are just some examples. Although some of the grain dishes we suggest may be new to you, they are all quite easy to prepare. Some grains, such as couscous, are available in precooked form. Follow the package directions for preparation, and then proceed with the recipe. Read the ingredients list on the label carefully, however, to avoid those products prepared with added salt. To give grain dishes extra flavor, use stock for the cooking liquid instead of water. You can also briefly sauté the grains in a small amount of unsalted butter or vegetable oil before adding the cooking liquid. This may add a few calories, but it also increases the flavor.

Creative salt-free cooking sometimes founders on salt-free breads. This is a difficult area, but one that is made easier by low-sodium baking powder. Found in most health-food stores, low-sodium baking powder works as well as ordinary baking powder; simply use one-and-a-half times as much. Low-sodium baking powder is used in many rewarding recipes in this chapter. In addition to satisfying breads, muffins, and rolls, there are also recipes for pizza and even for pretzels. The lack of salt will go almost unnoticed.

Orzo and Mushrooms

SERVES 4

SODIUM PER SERVING: 29 MG
CALORIES PER SERVING: 552

Orzo is versatile, small, rice-shaped pasta. It takes readily to seasonings and makes an excellent stuffing for poultry. Orzo cooks quickly and will become mushy if overcooked; keep an eye on the pot. In this recipe, any combination of fresh or soaked dried mushrooms can be used.

1½ cups orzo
½ cup olive oil
1 onion, thinly sliced
2 garlic cloves, minced
¾ cup coarsely chopped fresh parsley
12 ounces mushrooms, finely chopped
½ cup grated salt-free mozzarella cheese
¼ cup wine vinegar
freshly ground black pepper
1 tablespoon chopped fresh basil or 1 teaspoon dried

Cook the orzo *al dente*. Pour it into a colander and drain well. Rinse the orzo under warm water and drain again to remove as much water as possible. Put the orzo into a large serving bowl.

Heat the olive oil in a heavy skillet. Add the onion and garlic and cook over medium heat, stirring occasionally, for 5 minutes, or until the onion is soft. Add the parsley and cook, stirring occasionally, for 5 minutes longer. Add the mushrooms and cook, stirring occasionally, until the mushrooms just begin to brown, about 4 minutes. Add the mushroom mixture to the orzo.

Add the mozzarella and toss well. Add the wine vinegar and black pepper to taste and toss again. Garnish with the basil and serve at room temperature.

Spaghetti Primavera

SERVES 4

SODIUM PER SERVING: 20 MG
CALORIES PER SERVING: 612

The vegetables given in this recipe are usually available fresh in the spring and early summer, but almost any combination of fresh vegetables will be delicious.

2 tablespoons olive oil
2 tablespoons unsalted butter
2 garlic cloves, minced
3½ cups young zucchini
    or summer squash, cut into ¼-inch rounds
1½ cups whole leeks, cut into 2-inch pieces
2 cups stemmed whole cherry tomatoes
2 cups thin asparagus, cut into 2-inch pieces
2 tablespoons lemon juice
2 tablespoons red wine
1 cup spinach, torn into 2-inch pieces
3 tablespoons chopped fresh basil
2 tablespoons chopped fresh parsley
freshly ground black pepper
1 pound very thin spaghetti

Heat the oil and butter in a large, heavy skillet. Add the garlic, zucchini, leeks, cherry tomatoes, and asparagus and sauté over medium heat for 7 minutes or until the asparagus is tender. Add the lemon juice and red wine. Cook about 1½ minutes. Add the spinach, basil, parsley, and black pepper to taste. Mix well. Remove the skillet from the heat and cover.

Cook the spagetti *al dente*. When done, drain well and put into a large serving bowl. Add the vegetable mixture and toss gently. Serve warm or at room temperature.

Spaghetti with Fresh Tomato Sauce

SERVES 4

SODIUM PER SERVING: 32 MG
CALORIES PER SERVING: 635

Although this sauce is best made with fresh, ripe tomatoes, a 28-ounce can of salt-free, peeled, seeded, canned tomatoes can be substituted. Most imported canned tomatoes have no added salt. If canned tomatoes are used, cook the sauce for about 7 minutes longer.

3 pounds ripe tomatoes, blanched, peeled, seeded, and diced
2 tablespoons olive oil
2 tablespoons unsalted butter
1 large carrot, grated
1 medium-sized onion, diced
2 garlic cloves, minced
½ cup red wine
¾ cup chopped fresh basil
    or ½ cup chopped fresh parsley and 1 teaspoon dried basil
freshly ground black pepper
1 pound thin spaghetti

Blanch the tomatoes by placing them in a large pot of boiling water for about 10 seconds. Drain the tomatoes. When they are cool enough to handle, peel with a small sharp knife. Seed and chop the tomatoes, reserving the juice.

In a large heavy skillet, heat the olive oil and 3 tablespoons butter. Add the carrot, onion, and garlic. Sauté, stirring frequently, for 7 minutes, or until the carrot is soft. Add the chopped tomatoes and reserved juice. Cook over medium heat, stirring occasionally, for 10 minutes, or until the sauce begins to thicken. Add the red wine and cook for an additional 7 minutes. Add the basil and black pepper to taste. Stir well and remove skillet from heat.

Cook the spaghetti *al dente*. When it is done, drain well and put it into a large serving bowl. Add the remaining 1 tablespoon of butter and toss well. Pour half the sauce over the spaghetti and toss well. Then pour the remaining half of the sauce over the spaghetti and serve at once, garnished with additional basil if desired.

Linguini with Sweet Onions and Mozzarella

SERVES 4

SODIUM PER SERVING: 32 MG
CALORIES PER SERVING: 750

Sweet onions cooked slowly become even sweeter. If available, use Bermuda, large white, or vidalla onions for this recipe. Serve it as a main course with a salad or crisply cooked green vegetable, or serve it as a side dish with poached or baked fish.

2 tablespoons olive oil
1 large sweet onion, halved and thinly sliced
2 tablespoons chopped fresh parsley
   or ¾ teaspoon dried crushed thyme
⅛ teaspoon hot red pepper flakes
½ cup sweet vermouth
1 pound linguini
½ pound salt-free mozzarella cheese, grated

Heat the oil in a heavy skillet over medium heat. Add the onions, cover the skillet, and cook over low heat, stirring frequently, until the onions are amber-colored, about 20 to 25 minutes.

Add the parsley or thyme, hot red pepper flakes and vermouth to the onions. Cook for 5 minutes longer, stirring occasionally.

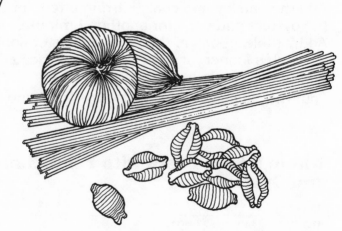

Cook the linguini *al dente.* When it is done, drain well and put into a large serving bowl. Pour the sauce over the pasta and toss gently. Top with the cheese and serve immediately.

Pasta with Oyster Sauce

SERVES 4

SODIUM PER SERVING: 92 MG
CALORIES PER SERVING: 613

Oysters are the lowest in sodium of any shellfish.
By cooking them quickly, they remain tender and juicy.
This sauce can also be served over rice.

1 pint (1½ cups) shucked fresh oysters
1 pound thin spaghetti
2 tablespoons olive oil
2 tablespoons unsalted butter
2 large garlic cloves, chopped
2 tablespoons chopped parsley
freshly ground black pepper

Cook the pasta *al dente.* When it is done, drain and transfer it to a serving bowl.

Drain the oysters and reserve the liquid.

Put the oil and butter into a small heavy saucepan. When the mixture starts to sizzle, add the garlic. Cook, stirring frequently, until the garlic is golden, about 4 to 5 minutes.

Add the parsley and cook, stirring often, for 2 minutes. Add the oysters and cook for another 2 minutes, stirring often. Add 2 tablespoons of the reserved oyster liquid and cook for 2 minutes longer, or until the sauce is heated through. Add black pepper to taste.

Pour the sauce over the pasta. Toss well and serve.

Whole Wheat Pasta with Pesto Sauce and Oysters

SERVES 4

SODIUM PER SERVING: 72 MG
CALORIES PER SERVING: 276

Pesto is a full-bodied sauce that goes particularly well with hearty whole wheat pasta. The basil flavor of the pesto is a good complement to the oysters. Use any type of whole wheat pasta in this recipe.

1 pound whole wheat pasta
1 tablespoon unsalted butter
1 pint shucked fresh oysters
½ cup Pesto Sauce with Walnuts (see page 29)

Cook the pasta *al dente*. Whole wheat pasta takes a little longer than regular pasta to cook.

While the pasta is cooking, melt the butter in a skillet over medium heat. Add the oysters and gently sauté until the edges of the oysters curl, about 1 to 2 minutes.

Drain the pasta well and put it into a large serving bowl. Add the pesto sauce and toss well. Pour the oysters over the pasta and toss gently. Serve hot or at room temperature.

Green Noodles with Sweet Red Pepper Sauce

SERVES 4

SODIUM PER SERVING: 86 MG
CALORIES PER SERVING: 383

Pasta made with spinach has a lovely green color. Make this dish with linguini or with such macaroni shapes as small shells. For a creamy sauce, toss the pasta with ¾ cup of salt-free ricotta cheese before adding the sauce.

4 sweet red peppers
2 tablespoons olive oil
1 cup chopped sweet onion
1 garlic clove
⅛ teaspoon hot red pepper flakes
¼ cup Vegetable Stock (see page 48)
¼ cup white wine
1 tablespoon wine vinegar
¼ cup fresh basil leaves
1 pound spinach pasta

Preheat the broiler.

Place the whole red peppers on a baking sheet and cook under the broiler, turning occasionally, until all sides are black. Remove the peppers from the broiler and put them into a paper bag. Close the bag and let stand until the peppers are cool enough to handle. Remove the skins, stems, and seeds and cut the peppers into strips.

In a large skillet, heat the oil over medium heat. When hot, add the onion, cover the skillet, and cook for 10 minutes, stirring frequently. Add the garlic and sauté until browned, about 5 minutes longer. Add the pepper strips, red pepper flakes, stock, wine, and vinegar. Cook for 5 minutes longer. Remove the skillet from the heat and let the pepper mixture cool to room temperature.

Put the pepper mixture and the basil into the container of a food processor or blender. Process until the ingredients are chopped and well blended, but not liquified.

Cook the pasta *al dente*. When it is done, drain it well and put it into a serving bowl. Top with the sweet red pepper sauce and toss well. Serve immediately or at room temperature.

Tomato, Mushroom, Chive, and Mozzarella Pizza Topping

TOPS 2 12-INCH PIZZAS

SODIUM PER RECIPE: 138 MG
CALORIES PER RECIPE: 824

2 cups salt-free tomato sauce
¾ cup sliced mushrooms
3 tablespoons chopped chives
1 cup shredded salt-free mozzarella cheese

Preheat the oven to 400°F.

Spread half the sauce evenly over each pizza. Top with half the mushrooms and 1½ tablespoons of the chives. Bake the pizza for 15 minutes.

Remove the pizza from the oven and top with the mozzarella cheese. Return the pizza to the oven and bake until the cheese melts and begins to bubble, about 10 minutes longer. Cut the pizza into wedges and serve immediately.

Whole Wheat Pizza

MAKES 2 12-INCH PIZZAS

SODIUM PER PIZZA: 12 MG
CALORIES PER PIZZA: 846

Pizza toppings are a good way to unleash your cooking creativity.
Almost anything goes.

1 envelope active dry yeast
1¼ cups lukewarm water
2 teaspoons olive oil
1½ cups whole wheat flour
2 cups unbleached white flour
¼ cup cornmeal
topping (see opposite page and page 124)

Put the yeast into a large bowl. Add the water, stir,
and set aside for 5 minutes to allow the yeast to dissolve.

Oil a large bowl with the olive oil.

Stir the whole wheat flour and the white flour into the
yeast mixture. Turn the dough out on a lightly floured
surface and knead until it is elastic, about 8 to 10 minutes.
Form the dough into a ball and put it into the oiled bowl,
turning the dough to coat it with the oil. Cover the dough
with a clean kitchen towel and let it rise in a warm place
for 2 hours.

Preheat the oven to 400°F. Sprinkle the cornmeal on two
12- or 14-inch round baking sheets or pizza pans.

Punch down the dough and divide it in half. Using a floured
rolling pin, roll the dough out on a lightly floured surface
until it is a circle 12 inches in diameter and ⅛-inch thick.
Repeat with the remaining dough.

Put the dough on the baking sheets or pizza pans. Top each
with half the topping. Let the pizzas rest for 10 minutes.

Put the pizzas in the oven and bake for 20 to 25 minutes.
Cut the pizzas into wedges and serve immediately.

Ricotta, Basil, and Tomato Pizza Topping

TOPS 2 12-INCH PIZZAS

SODIUM PER RECIPE: 70 MG
CALORIES PER RECIPE: 821

2 tablespoons olive oil
1 cup salt-free ricotta cheese
1 cup firmly packed basil leaves
freshly ground black pepper
2 medium-sized tomatoes, very thinly sliced
1 green pepper, seeded and cut into very thin rings

Preheat the oven to 400°F.

Brush 1 tablespoon of olive oil over each pizza.
Let rest for 10 minutes.
Bake the pizza dough for 15 minutes.

Process the ricotta, basil and black pepper to taste
in a food processor or blender until smooth.

Spread half the ricotta mixture evenly over each
partially cooked pizza. Arrange half the tomato
and pepper slices over the mixture.
Grind additional black pepper over the pizza.

Bake for 5 to 10 minutes longer.
Cut the pizza into wedges and serve immediately.

Alfredo Viazzi's Bucatini alla Savini

SERVES 4 TO 6

SODIUM PER SERVING: 82 MG
CALORIES PER SERVING: 802

Alfredo Viazzi is the owner of the renowned New York City restaurant
Trattoria Alfredo. He is the author of two cookbooks on Italian cooking,
Alfredo Viazzi's Cooking Book and *Cucina e Nostalgia*. Bucatini, the pasta
used in this dish, is long, thick, and hollow, rather like hollow spaghetti.

1/2 cup olive oil
3 medium-sized zucchini, sliced into 1/4-inch rounds
2 tablespoons unsalted butter
1/4 cup thinly sliced onion
1 garlic clove, minced
1 pound ground lamb
1/2 cup red wine
1/8 teaspoon grated nutmeg
freshly ground black pepper
3 cups salt-free tomato sauce
1 teaspoon finely chopped parsley
1 teaspoon chopped fresh basil
    or 1/4 teaspoon dried basil
2 mint leaves, chopped
    or 1/8 teaspoon dried mint
1 pound bucatini
1/2 cup grated salt-free cheese

Heat the oil in a skillet. Add the zucchini slices, a few at a time, and sauté until they are golden brown. Remove the slices from the skillet with a slotted spoon and drain in a single layer on paper towels.

Pour any oil remaining in the skillet into a saucepan. Add the butter and heat until the butter melts. Add the onion and garlic and sauté over medium heat until golden. Lower the heat and add the ground lamb. Cook the lamb, stirring frequently, until it is browned, about 7 minutes.

Add the wine to the saucepan. Stir well and simmer over low heat for 8 minutes. Add the nutmeg and black pepper to taste. Add the tomato sauce and mix well. Simmer, uncovered, for 15 minutes, stirring occasionally. Remove the saucepan from the heat and keep the sauce warm.

Cook the bucatini *al dente*. Drain well.

As the pasta cooks, melt the remaining butter in a skillet over low heat. Add the parsley, basil, mint, and zucchini and stir gently. Cook until the mixture is just hot through.

Toss the bucatini and the tomato sauce together in a large bowl. Top with the zucchini mixture. Serve immediately with the grated cheese on the side.

Pasta Salad with Salmon and Peas

SERVES 4

SODIUM PER SERVING: 122 MG
CALORIES PER SERVING: 646

An excellent dish for lunch or dinner on a warm day, this simple pasta
salad is easy to make. The light yogurt-dill dressing gives it a pleasantly
piquant flavor. All you need to make this a full meal is a fresh loaf of
crusty Italian bread, a green salad, fresh fruit, and perhaps a glass of
chilled white wine.

1 pound small pasta shells
2 cups Quick Poaching Stock (see page 22)
1 pound salmon steak
1 cup fresh shelled peas
3 whole scallions, chopped

Yogurt-Dill Dressing:

1 cup unflavored low-fat yogurt
2 tablespoons red wine vinegar
2 tablespoons Fish Stock (see page 49)
juice of ½ lemon
3 tablespoons chopped fresh dill
3 tablespoons chopped fresh chives
1 teaspoon salt-free Dijon-style mustard
freshly ground black pepper

Cook the pasta shells *al dente*. Since small pasta shapes
cook quickly, check often to avoid overcooking. Drain the
pasta and put it into a large serving bowl.

Put the poaching liquid into a medium-sized saucepan.
Bring it to a boil over medium heat. Add the salmon steak,
cover the saucepan, and simmer gently over low heat until
the salmon is done, about 7 minutes. Remove the fish from
the saucepan. Continue to simmer the poaching liquid until
it is reduced by half. Reserve the liquid. When the salmon is
cool enough to handle, remove the skin and bones and flake
the flesh with a fork. Discard the skin and bones.

Bring ½ cup of water to a boil in a small saucepan.
Add the peas and cook until just tender, about 5 minutes.
Drain the peas well.

In a small bowl, combine the yogurt, vinegar, reserved poaching liquid, lemon juice, dill, chives, mustard, and pepper to taste. Mix well. Pour the dressing over the pasta and toss thoroughly. Add the scallions, peas and salmon. Toss very gently. Set aside at for at least 30 minutes to allow the flavors to blend. Serve at room temperature. If this dish is made in advance, cover well and refrigerate until 1 hour before serving.

Bulgur Wheat Salad (Tabouleh)

SERVES 6

SODIUM PER SERVING: 7 MG
CALORIES PER SERVING: 279

Highly nutritious, bulgur is made of whole wheat berries that have been steamed and broken up. If the berries were ground instead, the result would be whole wheat flour. Bulgur salad is refreshing and easy to digest. It is best made when fresh mint is available. The amount of fresh mint can be increased to one cup if desired.

1 cup bulgur wheat
1¾ cups boiling water
½ cup finely chopped scallions
2 tomatoes, seeded and diced
½ cup chopped parsley
4 tablespoons chopped fresh mint
  or 2 teaspoons crushed dried mint
½ cup olive oil
¼ cup lemon juice
freshly ground black pepper

Put the bulgur into a large bowl and pour the boiling water over it. Stir well. Let the bulgur soak for 1 hour.

Drain the bulgur, squeezing out as much liquid as possible.

Add the scallions, tomatoes, parsley, mint, olive oil, and lemon juice. Add black pepper to taste. Toss well and serve.

Noodles with Peanut Sauce

SERVES 4 TO 6

SODIUM PER SERVING: 3 MG
CALORIES PER SERVING: 463

Served as a luncheon dish or as an appetizer, noodles with peanut sauce are unusual and delicious. This dish can be made in advance and stored, ungarnished, in the refrigerator, but be sure to remove it about 30 minutes before serving to allow it to warm to room temperature.

1 pound spaghetti, linguini or fettucini

Peanut Sauce:

3 tablespoons salt-free peanut butter
3 tablespoons water
1 teaspoon sugar
2 tablespoons balsamic vinegar
2 tablespoons sesame oil
2 garlic cloves, finely chopped (optional)
⅛ teaspoon cayenne pepper

Garnish:

2 tablespoons finely chopped scallions
3 tablespoons coarsely chopped unsalted peanuts
1 tablespoon chopped fresh coriander (optional)

Cook the pasta *al dente*. When it is done, empty it into a colander and rinse with cold water. Drain the pasta well and put it into a large serving bowl.

Put the peanut butter, water, sugar, balsamic vinegar, oil, garlic, and cayenne pepper into the container of a food processor or blender or into a mixing bowl. Blend well until the mixture is smooth.

Pour the sauce over the pasta and toss well. Garnish with the scallions, peanuts, and the coriander if desired.

Curried Noodles with Vegetables

SERVES 4

SODIUM PER SERVING: 78 MG
CALORIES PER SERVING: 646

By cooking the ingredients for this dish quickly, their flavors blend
yet each remains distinct. Use the best curry powder you can find.
For a vegetarian dish that is low in calories and rich in protein, substitute
1½ cups of diced bean curd (tofu) for the chicken. Cook the bean curd
for half the time you would the chicken.

5 to 7 medium-sized dried Oriental mushrooms
1 cup warm water
3 tablespoons safflower oil
4 whole scallions, trimmed and cut into 2-inch pieces
1 teaspoon chopped fresh ginger
1 whole chicken breast, skinned, boned, and cubed
3 garlic cloves, minced
¼ teaspoon hot red pepper flakes
¼ pound trimmed fresh snow peas
½ pound Chinese cabbage (bok choy), cut into 2-inch pieces
1 tablespoon balsamic vinegar
¼ cup unsalted roasted peanuts
1½ cups watercress, tough stems removed
1 tablespoon unsalted butter
1 tablespoon curry powder
1 tablespoon sesame oil
12 ounces fine egg noodles
2 tablespoons chopped fresh coriander

Put the dried mushrooms into a medium-sized bowl and
cover with 1 cup of warm water. Soak the mushrooms for
20 minutes or until they are soft. Strain off and reserve the
soaking liquid. Cut away the tough mushrooms stems
and dice the caps.

Heat 2 tablespoons of the safflower oil over medium
heat in a large skillet or wok. Add the scallions and ginger
and sauté, stirring constantly, for 1½ minutes. Add the
chicken and sauté, stirring constantly, for 1½ minutes.

Using a slotted spoon, remove the scallions, ginger and chicken pieces and set aside.

Add 2 tablespoons of safflower oil to the skillet or wok. Add the garlic and red pepper flakes and sauté, stirring constantly, for 30 seconds. Add the mushrooms and sauté, stirring constantly, for 1 minute. Add the snow peas and sauté, stirring constantly, for 2 minutes. Add the Chinese cabbage and saute, stirring constantly, for 30 seconds. Add the reserved mushroom liquid and the vinegar and cook, stirring constantly, for 1½ minutes. Add the peanuts and watercress. Stir until the watercress is slightly wilted, about 1½ minutes. Return the scallions, ginger, and chicken pieces to the skillet or wok and mix well. Continue to cook until the chicken is heated through, about 2 minutes longer.

Cook the egg noodles *al dente*. When done, drain well and put into a serving bowl.

To make the curry sauce, melt the butter in a small saucepan. Add the curry powder and cook over low heat, stirring constantly, for 1½ minutes. Add the sesame oil, stir, and remove the saucepan from the heat. Pour the sauce over the noodles and toss gently.

Pour the chicken and vegetables mixture over the curried noodles. Garnish with the chopped coriander and serve at once.

Couscous with Vegetable Stew

SERVES 6

SODIUM PER SERVING: 83 MG
CALORIES PER SERVING: 388

Couscous, which is presteamed cracked semolina wheat, is a staple
food in North Africa and many parts of the Middle East. This recipe
comes from Morocco. The light, fluffy grains are perfect for absorbing
seasonings and gravy. For an interesting change of pace, serve couscous
instead of rice or pasta with any sort of stew or sauce. Couscous is
available in either partially or completely precooked form. Follow the
directions on the package to determine the cooking time.

2 cups couscous
3 cups water or *Vegetable Stock (see page 48)*
¼ teaspoon crushed saffron threads
½ teaspoon ground ginger
¼ teaspoon cinnamon
⅛ teaspoon cayenne pepper
1 teaspoon freshly ground black pepper
1 medium-sized red onion, cut into 2-inch pieces
1 pound sweet potatoes or yams, peeled and cut into
  1-inch cubes
1 pound small turnips, peeled and cut into eighths
¾ pound carrots, peeled and cut into 2-inch pieces
1 pound zucchini, peeled and cut into 1-inch rounds
½ cup raisins
1 cup cooked chickpeas
½ teaspoon hot red pepper flakes

Cook the couscous, following the directions on the package
for preparation.

Put the water or vegetable stock into a large pot and bring
to a boil. Add the saffron, ginger, cinnamon, cayenne pepper,
black pepper, onion, sweet potatoes, turnips, and carrots.
Cover the pot and cook over medium heat for 20 minutes,
or until the turnips and carrots are soft. Add the zucchini,
raisins and chickpeas. Cook 10 minutes longer.

Serve over or with the couscous, garnished with hot red
pepper flakes.

Barley Casserole with Dried Mushrooms

SERVES 4 TO 6

SODIUM PER SERVING: 5 MG
CALORIES PER SERVING: 250

This hearty casserole goes particularly well with poultry or simple stews. It is a good substitute for rice or potatoes at any meal.

10 large dried Oriental mushrooms
2¼ cups warm water
½ cup red wine
1 cup pearl barley
1 tablespoon plus 1 teaspoon unsalted butter
1 tablespoon plus 1 teaspoon safflower oil
3 whole scallions
½ cup fresh shelled peas
2 teaspoons chopped fresh tarragon
  or ½ teaspoon dried
2 teaspoons chopped fresh mint
  or ½ teaspoon dried
freshly ground black pepper

Put the dried mushrooms into a medium-sized bowl and add 1¼ cups of the warm water. Soak the mushrooms for 20 minutes, or until they are soft. Strain off and reserve 1 cup of the soaking liquid and discard the rest. Cut away the tough mushrooms stems and dice the caps.

Put the mushroom soaking liquid into a medium-sized saucepan. Add the wine and the remaining 1 cup of warm water. Quickly bring the mixture to a boil. Add the barley and stir well. Cover the saucepan and lower the heat. Cook the barley over low heat for 20 minutes, or until it is tender and the liquid is absorbed.

Trim the scallions and cut them into 2-inch lengths.

Heat the butter and oil in a large skillet. Add the mushrooms, scallions, and peas. Cook over medium heat, stirring frequently, for 12 minutes, or until the scallions are soft. Add the tarragon, mint, and black pepper to taste. Add the barley to the skillet and toss well. Serve immediately.

Saffron Rice and Black Beans

SERVES 4

SODIUM PER SERVING: 24 MG
CALORIES PER SERVING: 479

This highly nutritious, vegetarian, main-course dish is a Latin American favorite. Serve it with a simple green salad or an avocado salad.

1 cup dried black beans
2 cups water
1 medium-sized onion, halved
2 bay leaves
3 garlic cloves
1 cup rice
¼ teaspoon saffron threads

Garnish:

3 tomatoes, seeded and diced
1 cup diced sweet onion
3 tablespoons olive oil
1 tablespoon wine vinegar
½ teaspoon ground cumin
freshly ground black pepper
⅛ teaspoon cayenne pepper
3 tablespoons chopped fresh parsley
    or basil or ½ teaspoon dried

Rinse and sort the beans. Put them into a heavy pot and cover with 2 cups of water. Bring the water to a boil, cover the pot, and remove from the heat. Set aside and allow the beans to soak for 1 to 2 hours.

Add the onion, bay leaves, and garlic to the pot.
Put the pot over low heat and cook the beans, covered, for 1½ hours, or until they are tender. Add more water if necessary. Remove and discard the onion, bay leaves, and garlic when the beans are cooked. Keep the beans warm.

Prepare the tomato and onion garnish about 1 hour before serving. Put the tomatoes and onion into a serving bowl. Add the olive oil, vinegar, cumin, black pepper to taste, cayenne pepper and parsley or basil. Toss well.

Bring two cups of water to a boil in a saucepan and add the rice and saffron threads. Stir and cover the saucepan. Reduce the heat and cook for 18 to 20 minutes, or until the rice has absorbed all the water.

To serve, put the warm rice, the black beans, and the tomato garnish into separate bowls. Each diner should top a bed of rice with the beans and then with the garnish.

Chutney Rice

SERVES 4

SODIUM PER SERVING: 4 MG
CALORIES PER SERVING: 194

Serve this unusual, golden rice dish with grilled or roasted meat or fish. It is especially delicious with Charcoal-Grilled Indian Lamb (see page 93). If you can find it, use Indian basmati rice, which has a sweet, nutty flavor.

2 cups cooked rice
1 large apple, peeled, cored, and diced
1 small navel orange, peeled, white pith removed,
    and cut into small chunks
2 tablespoons chopped onion
3 tablespoons slivered almonds
3 tablespoons lemon juice
3 tablespoons chopped Apple Ginger Chutney (see page 32)
2 tablespoons chopped fresh coriander or dill

Put the rice into a serving bowl. Add the apple, onion, orange and almonds and toss well. Add the lemon juice and chutney and toss again. Set aside for 1 hour to allow the flavors to blend.

Serve at room temperature, garnished with the chopped coriander.

Brown Rice Pilaf

SERVES 4 TO 6

SODIUM PER SERVING: 14 MG
CALORIES PER SERVING: 257

Although it takes longer to cook brown rice, it is nutritionally superior to ordinary white rice — and it never gets sticky. Try serving this pilaf instead of the usual white rice dishes. This dish can be cooked in a 350°F. oven instead of on the stovetop.

2 tablespoons vegetable oil
1 tablespoon unsalted butter
1 small onion, diced
¼ teaspoon crushed dried rosemary
1 carrot, peeled and grated
1 cup brown rice
2 garlic cloves, minced
3 tablespoons slivered almonds
2½ cups water
1 medium-sized apple, peeled, cored and diced
juice of ½ lemon
3 tablespoons chopped parsley
zest of 1 lemon

Put the oil and butter into a heavy pot that has a tightly fitting lid. Melt the butter over medium heat. Add the onion, rosemary and carrot. Sauté, stirring frequently, for 7 minutes or until carrot is soft. Add the brown rice and garlic and cook, stirring frequently, for an additional 3 minutes.
Add the almonds and the water and stir well. Bring the mixture to the boil. Cover the pot tightly and reduce the heat to low. Cook for 50 minutes, or until rice is tender.

In a small bowl, combine the apple, lemon juice, parsley, and lemon zest. Blend well. When the rice is done, fold in the apple mixture and serve.

Basic Bread

MAKES 1 LARGE LOAF OR 2 SMALL LOAVES

SODIUM PER RECIPE: 146 MG
CALORIES PER RECIPE: 2,016

This bread has a rich, full flavor, with none of the "flatness" often associated with salt-free baking. Bake this bread in one large loaf pan, two small loaf pans, a French bread pan, or shape it into a loaf on a baking sheet.

1 package active dry yeast
1½ teaspoons sugar
¼ cup very warm water
1 cup low-fat milk
2 tablespoons vegetable oil
3½ to 4 cups unbleached white flour
¼ cup wheat germ (optional)

Put the yeast and sugar into a large bowl. Add the water, stir, and set aside for 5 minutes to allow the yeast to dissolve.

Add the milk and vegetable oil and stir well. Add the flour to the liquid, 1 cup at a time, mixing well after each addition. Add the wheat germ if you are using it. When the dough is no longer sticky, form it into a ball and let it rest in the bowl for 10 minutes.

Turn the dough out onto a lightly floured surface. Knead it well for 10 minutes.

Put the kneaded dough into a lightly greased bowl and cover it with a clean kitchen towel. Set aside in a warm place until the dough has doubled in bulk, about 1 hour.

Punch down the dough. Turn it out onto a lightly floured surface and shape it into 1 large loaf or 2 smaller loaves. Cut 3 diagonal slashes across the top of each loaf to allow the steam to escape. Put the loaves into well-greased loaf pans or on a greased baking sheet. Cover the loaves with a clean kitchen towel and set them aside in a warm place until they have risen by one-third their bulk, about 45 minutes.

Preheat the oven to 400°F. Bake the loaves for 20 minutes. Reduce the oven temperature to 350°F. and bake until the loaves are golden brown on top and sound hollow when tapped, about 20 to 30 minutes longer. Remove the loaves from the pans and cool on wire racks.

Onion Bread

MAKES 1 LOAF

SODIUM PER RECIPE: 210 MG
CALORIES PER RECIPE: 2,414

This variation on basic bread has a lovely swirl of green in each slice.

1 recipe for Basic Bread (see opposite page)

Filling:

2 tablespoons unsalted butter
2 cups chopped sweet onion
1 cup finely chopped parsley
1 tablespoon red wine vinegar
freshly ground black pepper
2 teaspoons poppy seeds

Prepare the bread dough as explained on the previous page. While the dough is rising, prepare the filling.
Melt the butter in a large skillet over medium heat.
Add the onions and cook, stirring frequently, for 15 minutes.
Add the vinegar and black pepper to taste. Cook for 3 to 5 minutes longer. Remove the skillet from the heat and stir in the parsley and poppy seeds.
Grease a 9x5x3-inch loaf pan.
When the dough has risen, punch it down. Turn the dough out onto a lightly floured surface and knead it again for 3 minutes. Using a floured rolling pin, roll out the dough into a rectangle that is 9x20 inches.
Spread the onion and parsley filling evenly over the dough, leaving a ½-inch border all around. Roll the dough up, jelly-roll-fashion, to make a 9-inch loaf. Put the loaf, seam-side down, into the loaf pan. Cut 3 diagonal slashes across the top of the loaf to allow the steam to escape. Cover the loaf with a clean kitchen towel and set it aside in a warm place until it has risen by one-third its bulk, about 45 minutes.
Preheat the oven to 400°F. Bake the loaf for 20 minutes. Reduce the oven temperature to 350°F. and bake until the loaf is golden brown on top and sounds hollow when tapped, about 20 to 30 minutes longer. Remove the loaf from the pans and cool on a wire rack.

James Beard's Black Pepper Bread with Rosemary

MAKES 2 LOAVES

SODIUM PER LOAF: 292 MG
CALORIES PER LOAF: 1,583

James Beard is the dean of American cooking. His many books, including *Beard on Bread* and *Beard on Pasta*, are authoritative guides to the culinary arts — and pleasurable reading as well. This fabulous bread was created by Mr. Beard for this book. The black pepper must be freshly ground.

½ cup warm water (110°F.)
2 packages active dry yeast
2 cups buttermilk
1 tablespoon freshly ground black pepper
1½ teaspoons chopped fresh rosemary
*   or ¾ teaspoon dried crumbled rosemary*
¼ cup melted unsalted butter
5½ cups flour

Egg wash:

1 egg yolk
2 tablespoons milk

Put the warm water into a small bowl. Sprinkle the yeast over the water and let stand for 1 to 2 minutes. Stir the mixture until the yeast is dissolved, then let stand again until the mixture is creamy.

Put the yeast mixture, buttermilk, pepper, rosemary, and butter into the bowl of an electric mixer. With the dough hook in place and the mixer on the lowest speed, add the flour, ½ cup at a time, until the dough is smooth and pulls away from the sides of the bowl.

Remove the dough from the mixing bowl. Put it on a lightly floured surface and knead, adding additional flour if necessary, until the dough is smooth and satiny.

Butter a large bowl. Form the dough into a ball and put it into the bowl, turning to coat the dough with the butter. Cover the bowl with a clean kitchen towel and let the dough rise for 1½ hours. Punch the dough down, cover it again, and allow it to rise again until it is doubled in bulk, about 1 hour longer.

Butter two 9x5x3-inch bread pans.

Remove the dough from the bowl. Divide it into two loaves and put them into the buttered pans. Cover the loaves with clean kitchen towels and let rise until the dough reaches the top of the pans, about 1 hour.

Preheat the oven to 375°F.

In a small bowl, make the egg wash by beating the egg yolk together with the milk. Slash the tops of the loaves down the center with a sharp knife. Brush the loaves with the egg wash. Bake until the loaves sound hollow when rapped with the knuckles, about 45 to 50 minutes. Remove the loaves from the oven. Turn them out onto a wire rack to cool.

Herbed Biscuits

MAKES 12 BISCUITS

SODIUM PER BISCUIT: 6 MG
CALORIES PER BISCUIT: 111

These light, flaky biscuits can be served with almost any meal. Use any fresh chopped herbs that you have on hand. Alternatively, add a teaspoon or so of coarsely ground black pepper for a biscuit with bite.

2 cups unbleached flour
4½ teaspoons low-sodium baking powder
4 tablespoons unsalted butter, softened
½ cup low-fat milk
3 tablespoons chopped fresh parsley, basil, dill or chervil

Preheat the oven to 400°F. Lightly grease a baking sheet.

In a mixing bowl, sift together the flour and baking powder. Mix in the butter with a fork until it is completely combined. Stir in the milk and chopped herbs, a little at a time, until the dough is soft but not sticky. (This may take a little more or less than ½ cup.)

Turn the dough out onto a lightly floured surface.
Handling the dough as little as possible, knead it quickly.
Roll the dough out with a floured rolling pin until it is about
½-inch thick.

Using a biscuit cutter or a glass with a diameter of about
1½ inches, cut biscuits out of the dough. Put the biscuits on
the baking sheet and bake until they are lightly browned,
about 15 minutes. Serve hot.

Hot Shot Corn Muffins

MAKES 12 MUFFINS

SODIUM PER MUFFIN: 17 MG
CALORIES PER MUFFIN: 102

This recipe can also be used to make a whole cornbread. Prepare the
batter, but leave out the barbecue sauce. Spoon half the batter into a
greased 8x8-inch baking pan. Gently spread the barbecue sauce on top
of the batter. Top with the remaining batter, being careful not to disturb
the layer of barbecue sauce. Bake the cornbread at 425°F. until golden on
top, about 25 minutes.

1 teaspoon unsalted butter, softened
1½ cups yellow cornmeal
½ cup whole wheat flour
4½ teaspoons low-sodium baking powder
1 cup low-fat milk
1 egg, beaten
1 tablespoon vegetable oil
3 tablespoons Barbecue Sauce (see page 30)

Preheat the oven to 425°F.
Lightly grease 12 muffin-tin cups with the butter.

In a mixing bowl combine the cornmeal, whole wheat flour, and baking powder. Add the milk, egg, oil and barbecue sauce. Stir well but do not overmix — muffin batter should be a little lumpy.

Spoon the batter into the muffin cups and bake until browned on top, about 15 to 20 minutes.

Indian Puffed Bread

MAKES 5 BREADS

SODIUM PER BREAD: 1 MG
CALORIES PER BREAD: 80

This bread from India is not only salt-free but shortening-free as well. Serve it as an hôrs d'oeuvre, with soup, or with salads. If you're cooking outdoors, cook it on the grill.

1 cup whole wheat flour
½ cup water

In a mixing bowl combine the flour with ¼ cup of the water. Mix well. Slowly mix in the remaining water. The dough will be stiff.

Turn the dough out onto a lightly floured surface and knead for about 12 minutes. Form the dough into a ball and put it back into a mixing bowl. Cover the dough with a damp, clean kitchen towel and set aside for 30 minutes.

Divide the dough into 5 balls. With a floured rolling pin, roll each ball out on a lightly floured surface to form a 6-inch disk. Cover the disks with a damp, clean kitchen towel as they are made.

Heat a well-seasoned or nonstick skillet over medium-high heat. When the skillet is very hot, put one disk into it. Shake the bread back and forth for about 1 minute as it cooks. Turn the bread and cook the other side, shaking it back and forth as it cooks.

To make the bread puff, press it for 2 seconds in several places with a spatula just before removing it from the skillet. The bread will puff when the spatula is lifted. Serve immediately.

Whole Wheat Pretzels

MAKES 30 PRETZELS

SODIUM PER PRETZEL: 3 MG
CALORIES PER PRETZEL: 69

Whole wheat pretzels are delicious as a satisfying snack by themselves or with drinks. The seeds on top add flavor and interest, but they can be omitted. For a more highly seasoned pretzel, add more black pepper or eat them as they do in Philadelphia, with mustard.

1 package active dry yeast
1½ teaspoons sugar
1½ cups very warm water
2¼ cups whole wheat flour
2¼ cups all-purpose flour
2 tablespoons caraway or sesame seeds
1 tablespoon freshly ground black pepper
1 egg, beaten

Preheat the oven to 400°F. Lightly grease a baking sheet.

Put the yeast and sugar into a large bowl. Add the water, stir, and set aside for 5 minutes to allow the yeast to dissolve.

Stir the whole wheat flour and the all-purpose flour into the yeast mixture. Knead in half the caraway or sesame seeds and all the black pepper. Turn the dough out onto a lightly floured surface and knead until the dough is elastic, about 8 to 10 minutes.

Divide the dough into 30 pieces, each roughly 2 inches in diameter. Roll the pieces out into strips about 8 inches long and ½ inch wide. To form the pretzels, bring the ends of each strip toward the center of the strip, forming two loops. The ends should cross, with one end in front and the other behind, where they meet at the center and should project about ½-inch below the center of the strip. Pinch together where the ends cross.

Put the pretzels on the baking sheet. Brush them lightly with the beaten egg and sprinkle with the remaining caraway or sesame seeds. Bake until the pretzels are lightly browned, about 20 to 25 minutes. Cool the pretzels completely on wire racks. Store them in a tightly covered container.

Vegetables

There are no vegetables more delicious than those just picked from our own gardens. We handle them carefully, from the gentle scrubbing under cold water to the brief steaming over hot water. They are then tossed lightly with a tiny bit of sweet butter and a sprinkling of fresh herbs, and eaten slowly. What could be better?

Unfortunately, even those of us with large gardens must often buy our vegetables. Take the time to learn about and seek out fresh, high-quality produce. You will be rewarded with greater flavor and food value.

Looks can be deceiving in vegetables. For example, happy as you may be to see peas in the pod at the supermarket, remember that their frozen counterparts probably taste sweeter and less starchy. The frozen peas may have retained more vitamins in the flash-freezing process than are in the "fresh" peas, which were probably picked more than three days before very far from your supermarket. Bigger is not necessarily better in vegetables. Thin young zucchini are preferable to the seed-laden monsters some gardeners grow. Remember, too, that artificial-looking color in vegetables generally indicates a certain unnaturalness in the way they were grown. Vegetables specially bred for shelf-life considerations and shipping strength are vegetables to be avoided. Vegetables which have the primary virtue of fitting exactly into cellophane-wrapped packages have relatively less food value and certainly less flavor.

Vegetables are important sources of vitamins and dietary fiber, but to get the maximum benefit they should be cooked as little as possible as quickly as possible. The best way to lock in the nutrients is by steaming or stir-frying. The old-fashioned practice of blanching vegetables in a lot of boiling water and then plunging them in ice water enhances color, but significantly reduces nutritional value.

Some vegetables are much higher in natural sodium than others, but unless you are on a medically restricted diet, celery, beets, carrots, kale, spinach, and artichokes will probably do no harm. And these same vegetables are high in important nutrients.

Preparing vegetables without salt often requires some compensation in seasoning. Simply steamed fresh vegetables such as broccoli are much enhanced by some chopped garlic and parsley sauteed in sweet butter and sprinkled on top. In general, fresh herbs, freshly ground black pepper, and lemon juice will enhance any vegetable. The variety of recipes in this chapter will give you many other ideas as well.

Sesame Green Beans

SERVES 4 TO 6

SODIUM PER SERVING: 9 MG
CALORIES PER SERVING: 71

Freshly toasted sesame seeds are a delicious seasoning. It only takes a minute or two to toast them. This dish goes well with fish steaks, veal stew and poultry dishes.

1 pound fresh green beans, trimmed
2 tablespoons sesame seeds
1 tablespoon unsalted butter
freshly ground black pepper

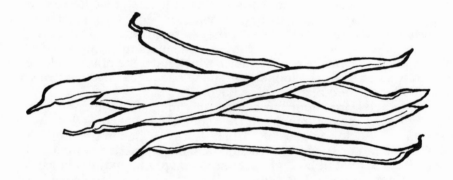

Steam the green beans until they are tender but still crisp, about 4 to 5 minutes. Rinse them with cold water and drain well.

Place a large, ungreased skillet over medium heat. When it is hot, add the sesame seeds and toast, stirring often, until the seeds are browned. Add the butter and stir to coat the sesame seeds.

When the butter is completely melted, add the green beans to the skillet and toss well. Serve hot.

Green Beans with Slivered Mushrooms

SERVES 4

SODIUM PER SERVING: 21 MG
CALORIES PER SERVING: 60

¾ pound fresh green beans, trimmed
2 tablespoons salt-free Dijon-style mustard
1 tablespoon lemon juice
¼ pound white mushrooms, thinly sliced
2 tablespoons chopped fresh dill or parsley

Steam the green beans until they are tender but still
crisp, about 4 to 5 minutes. Rinse them with cold water,
drain well, and put them into a serving dish.
Add the mushrooms.

Combine the mustard and lemon juice in a small bowl.
Add to the green beans and mushrooms and toss gently.
Sprinkle with the chopped dill or parsley and serve at
room temperature.

Orange Beets

SERVES 4 TO 6

SODIUM PER SERVING: 110 MG
CALORIES PER SERVING: 192

Orange beets are good served at room temperature as a salad
or as a vegetable course.

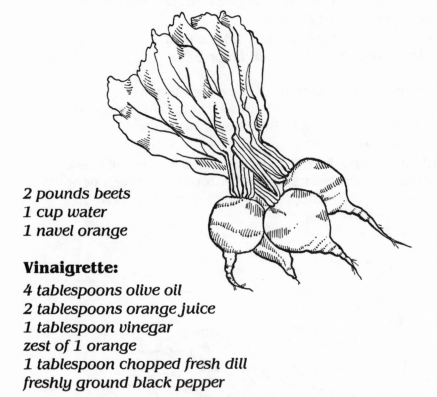

2 pounds beets
1 cup water
1 navel orange

Vinaigrette:

4 tablespoons olive oil
2 tablespoons orange juice
1 tablespoon vinegar
zest of 1 orange
1 tablespoon chopped fresh dill
freshly ground black pepper

Preheat the oven to 350°F.

Scrub the beets and remove the rootlets and tops,
leaving about 1½ inches of stem. Put the beets into a
baking dish with the water. Bake until the beets are tender,
about 45 minutes to 1 hour. When the beets are cool
enough to handle, peel them and slice them into ¼-inch
rounds. Put the slices into a serving dish.

Peel the orange, removing as much of the white pith as
possible. Cut the orange crosswise into very thin rounds,
then cut each round into quarters.

In a small bowl, combine the olive oil, orange juice, vinegar, orange zest, dill, and black pepper to taste. Mix well and pour over the beets. Toss well and garnish with the orange pieces.

Baby Beets and Turnips

SERVES 4

SODIUM PER SERVING: 113 MG
CALORIES PER SERVING: 109

Delicate young beets and turnips have a marvellously fresh flavor. They cook quickly — so be careful not to overcook them.

8 baby beets, approximately 1½ inches in diameter
8 baby turnips, approximately 1½ inches in diameter
1 tablespoon unsalted butter
1 medium-sized sweet onion, cut into eighths
2 teaspoons vinegar or lemon juice
freshly ground black pepper

Scrub the beets and turnips under running water. Remove and reserve the tops. Put the beets and turnips into boiling water in separate small saucepans. Cover each saucepan and cook until the vegetables are just tender, about 5 minutes for the turnips and 8 minutes for the beets. Drain the vegetables and peel them if desired. Put the vegetables into separate bowls (so the beets won't make the turnips pink), add ½ tablespoon of the butter to each one, and toss to coat the vegetables. Set aside and keep warm.

Coarsely chop the reserved tops and the onion. Put them into a steamer basket over boiling water and steam until tender, about 2 to 3 minutes. Put the mixture into a bowl and add the vinegar or lemon juice and black pepper to taste. Blend well.

Make a bed of the greens and onion mixture on a small serving platter. Top with the beets and turnips. Grind black pepper to taste over the vegetables. Serve immediately or at room temperature.

Broccoli with Oriental Mushrooms

SERVES 4 TO 6

SODIUM PER SERVING: 84 MG
CALORIES PER SERVING: 151

The robust flavor of the stir-fried broccoli is a good complement to a simple main dish such as poached chicken breasts. If you use the sesame oil, add it just before the broccoli is ready.

6 medium-sized dried Oriental mushrooms
1 medium-sized head broccoli
4 tablespoons vegetable oil
1 tablespoon chopped ginger
4 garlic cloves, chopped
3 whole scallions, chopped
½ sweet red pepper, seeded and cut into 2-inch slivers
3 tablespoons balsamic vinegar
1 teaspoon sesame oil (optional)
2 tablespoons chopped coriander
  or parsley

Soak the dried mushrooms in a bowl of warm water until soft, about 20 minutes. Strain off the liquid, reserving ¼ cup. Cut away any tough stems and slice the mushrooms thinly. Set aside.

Cut the broccoli into flowerettes. Peel the stems and slice them thinly into diagonal pieces. Set aside.

Heat 2 tablespoons of the vegetable oil in a wok or large skillet over medium-high heat. When the oil is very hot, add the ginger, garlic, scallions, and mushrooms. Sauté, stirring constantly, for 2 to 3 minutes. Remove the ingredients with a slotted spoon and set aside.

Add the remaining oil to the wok or skillet. Add the broccoli stems and sauté, stirring constantly, for about 2 minutes. Add the flowerettes and continue to sauté, stirring constantly, for 5 minutes longer. Be careful not to burn the broccoli; add more oil if necessary.

Add the reserved mushroom liquid and cover the wok or skillet. Steam until the broccoli is tender, about 3 minutes. Uncover and stir in the reserved ginger, garlic, scallions and mushrooms. Add the vinegar or soy sauce and cook for 2 minutes longer. Add the sesame oil (if you are using it) and stir well. Sprinkle with coriander and serve immediately.

Broccoli and Oranges in Vinaigrette

SERVES 4 TO 6

SODIUM PER SERVING: 29 MG
CALORIES PER SERVING: 228

The citrus flavor combines nicely with the broccoli in this dish. If fresh chives are not available, use the chopped tops of scallions instead.

6 cups broccoli flowerettes
2 small navel oranges
2 tablespoons chopped chives

Vinaigrette:

3 tablespoons balsamic vinegar
6 tablespoons olive oil
2 tablespoons orange juice
freshly ground black pepper
1 garlic clove, minced

Steam the broccoli over boiling water until just tender, about 3 to 5 minutes.

Peel the oranges, removing as much of the white pith as possible. Slice the oranges into thin rounds and then cut each round into quarters.

Put the broccoli and orange pieces into a serving bowl.

In a small bowl, combine the vinegar, olive oil, orange juice, black pepper to taste, and garlic. Mix well. Pour the vinaigrette over the broccoli and oranges and toss well. Set aside for an hour to allow flavors to blend. Sprinkle with chives and serve at room temperature.

Brussels Sprouts with Apples

SERVES 4 TO 6

SODIUM PER SERVING: 14 MG
CALORIES PER SERVING: 114

The nuts and apples in this dish add texture to the sprouts.
Walnuts are preferred for their low sodium content. This is a good
dish to serve with a Holiday Roast Turkey (see page 109).

1 pound fresh Brussels sprouts
1 large apple, peeled, cored, and sliced
1 tablespoon unsalted butter
2 tablespoons chopped parsley
3 tablespoons chopped walnuts
1 teaspoon lemon juice
freshly ground black pepper

Wash and trim the Brussels sprouts. Cut an *X* into the
bottom of each one with a small sharp knife.

Put the Brussels sprouts into a pot containing 2 inches
of boiling water. Cook until tender, about 7 minutes.
Drain well.

Put the butter and apple into a small saucepan.
Put the Brussels sprouts on top of the apple.
Cover the saucepan and cook, shaking the saucepan
occasionally, until the apple has softened,
about 5 minutes.

Put the apple and Brussels sprouts into a serving dish.
Garnish with the parsley, walnuts, lemon juice, and black
pepper to taste. Serve immediately.

Cabbage with Fresh Herbs

SERVES 4 TO 6

SODIUM PER SERVING: 39 MG
CALORIES PER SERVING: 87

Young cabbage has a mild, almost sweet flavor and should be cooked quickly so it is still fairly crisp when served.

1 small head cabbage
2 tablespoons unsalted butter
½ cup chopped parsley or *dill* or *chives*

Discard the tough outer leaves of the cabbage.
Cut it into small wedges and remove the core.
Put the wedges into a steamer over boiling water and cover tightly. Steam over medium heat until the cabbage is just tender, about 5 minutes.

Transfer the cabbage to a serving dish. Dot with butter, sprinkle with the parsley, dill, or chives, and serve.

Meatless Chili

SERVES 4 TO 6

SODIUM PER SERVING: 26 MG
CALORIES PER SERVING: 336

Served with rice, this chili is a fine main dish for a satisfying
vegetarian meal. Vary the amount of cayenne pepper to taste,
but go easy with it. It's very hot. For extra hotness, add seeded and
chopped green chili peppers. Avoid commercial chili powders —
almost all of them contain salt.

2 tablespoons vegetable oil
1½ cups chopped onion
3 garlic cloves, minced
¾ teaspoon dried oregano
1 teaspoon ground cumin
1 16-ounce can salt-free whole tomatoes
⅔ cup Barbecue Sauce (see page 30)
4 cups cooked kidney beans
⅛ teaspoon cayenne pepper
½ cup grated low-sodium Cheddar or Monterey Jack cheese

Heat the vegetable oil in a large, heavy skillet.
When the oil is hot, add 1 cup of the chopped onion,
the garlic, oregano, and cumin. Sauté until the onion is
tender, about 8 minutes.

Drain the tomatoes and reserve the liquid. Chop the
tomatoes coarsely and add, along with the reserved liquid,
to the onion mixture. Add the barbecue sauce. Mix well and
simmer over low heat for 15 minutes.

Add the beans and simmer gently for 15 to 20 minutes
longer. Add the cayenne pepper. Serve over rice, topped
with the cheese and garnished with the remaining
chopped onion.

Lemon Ginger Carrots

SERVES 4 TO 6

SODIUM PER SERVING: 43 MG
CALORIES PER SERVING: 59

For an interesting variation of this recipe, use ½ pound of carrots and ½ pound of parsnips.

1 pound carrots
1 tablespoon unsalted butter, softened
½ teaspoon grated ginger
½ teaspoon lemon juice
1 teaspoon chopped fresh coriander or tarragon
  or 2 teaspoons chopped parsley

Peel and trim the carrots. Cut them into diagonal slices about ½ inch thick and 2 inches long.

Steam the carrots over boiling water until just tender, about 8 to 10 minutes.

In a large bowl, combine the butter, ginger, lemon juice, and herbs. Blend well. Add the carrots and toss. Serve immediately.

Herbed Whole Cauliflower

SERVES 4 TO 6

SODIUM PER SERVING: 53 MG
CALORIES PER SERVING: 165

This is an attractive, dramatic way to present a whole head of cauliflower. Be sure not to overcook the cauliflower; if you do, it will be bitter and mushy.

1 whole cauliflower, trimmed
2 tablespoons unsalted butter
3 garlic cloves, minced
¼ cup chopped parsley
3 tablespoons chopped fresh basil or 3 teaspoons dried
1 cup unflavored bread crumbs
freshly ground black pepper

Trim the end of the cauliflower so that it will stand in a steamer basket. Add 1 cup of water to the steamer, cover tightly, and steam the whole cauliflower over boiling water until just tender, about 15 to 20 minutes. Remove from the steamer and keep warm.

Melt the butter in a saucepan over medium heat.
Add the garlic and sauté until just golden, about 5 minutes. Add the parsley, basil, bread crumbs, and black pepper to taste. Sauté until the bread crumbs are browned, about 5 minutes longer.

Place the cauliflower on a serving platter and pour the herbed bread crumb mixture over the top. Serve at once.

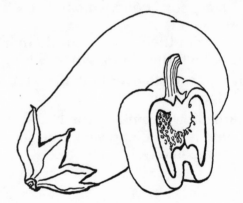

Grilled Eggplant

SERVES 4

SODIUM PER SERVING: 4 MG
CALORIES PER SERVING: 153

This simple way to cook eggplant is also one of the best.
Serve it with any grilled food or as a first course at lunch or dinner.

1 medium-sized eggplant, cut into ½-inch rounds
¼ cup olive oil
3 tablespoons diced sweet onions or shallots
2 tablespoons chopped fresh parsley
  or basil or 1 teaspoon dried
2 tablespoons wine vinegar or lemon juice

Preheat the broiler or grill to high.

If dried herbs are being used, add the herbs to the olive oil and mix well.

Brush both sides of each eggplant slice with the olive oil. Place the rounds directly on the grill or in a broiler pan six inches from the heat.

Cook the eggplant until brown and tender, about 7 minutes on each side.

Put the eggplant slices into a serving dish and top with the onion or shallots and fresh herbs, if used. Drizzle any remaining oil over the slices and sprinkle with the vinegar or lemon juice. Serve at room temperature.

Eggplant Pizza

SERVES 4

SODIUM PER SERVING: 16 MG
CALORIES PER SERVING: 276

When served with a salad and a crusty bread, this is an excellent luncheon or supper dish.

1 large eggplant, about 1 pound
1/4 cup olive oil
1 large ripe tomato
1/4 pound unsalted mozzarella cheese
3 tablespoons chopped sweet onion
1 tablespoon chopped fresh basil or 1 teaspoon dried

Preheat the broiler to high.

Cut the eggplant lengthwise into 3/4-inch slices. Put the slices on a broiler pan and brush with half of the olive oil. Broil about 6 inches from the heat until browned on top, about 7 minutes. Turn the eggplant slices and brush the other sides with the remaining oil. Broil until browned, about 5 minutes longer. Remove the pan from the broiler.

Cut the tomato into 1/2-inch slices, then cut each slice in half. Cut the mozzarella into 1/4-inch slices.

Place the tomato slices on the eggplant slices. Top with the mozzarella slices. Sprinkle the onion and basil over the cheese. Return the eggplant to the broiler and broil until the cheese is melted, about 3 to 5 minutes.

Braised and Marinated Leeks

SERVES 4

SODIUM PER SERVING: 4 MG
CALORIES PER SERVING: 72

Marinated leeks are a fine first course. They can also be served at room temperature with fish, poultry, or meat dishes. If sweet red peppers are not available, add ½ cup diced carrots to the leeks when they are half cooked.

3 to 4 large leeks
1 lemon
⅓ cup Vegetable Stock (see page 48)
  or Chicken Stock (see page 50)
½ sweet red pepper, seeded and diced
1½ tablespoons olive oil
1½ tablespoons lemon juice
2 tablespoons chopped fresh parsley
freshly ground black pepper

Trim away and discard two-thirds of the green parts of the leeks and cut off the root end. Slice each leek lengthwise and rinse thoroughly to remove all the grit.

Grate the zest from half the lemon. Remove all the remaining peel and white pith from the lemon. Cut the lemon into paper-thin slices and reserve.

Put the leeks into a saucepan and add the stock. Simmer, covered, until the leeks are tender, about 15 minutes. Let the leeks cool in the stock. When they are cool, drain the leeks, reserving the stock. Place the leeks on a serving platter and top with the diced red pepper.

In a small bowl, combine the olive oil, lemon juice, black pepper, lemon zest, and parsley. Add 1 tablespoon of the reserved stock. Mix well and pour over the leeks and red pepper. Garnish with the lemon slices. Let stand for 1 hour or longer at room temperature before serving.

Mushroom Melange

SERVES 4

SODIUM PER SERVING: 15 MG
CALORIES PER SERVING: 147

The dried Oriental mushrooms give this dish texture and rich flavor. It goes very well with pasta and grain dishes. For an elegant first course, serve the mushrooms on thinly sliced toast.

6 dried Oriental mushrooms
2 tablespoons olive oil
3 garlic cloves, chopped
12 ounces fresh white mushrooms, thickly sliced
2 tablespoons red wine
¼ teaspoon nutmeg
hot red pepper flakes
freshly ground black pepper
2 tablespoons chopped fresh basil or parsley
2 tablespoons pine nuts

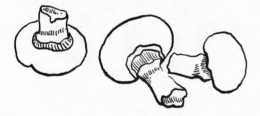

Rinse the dried mushrooms. Put them into a bowl and add warm water to cover. Soak the mushrooms until softened. Drain them well and pat dry. Discard the tough stems and cut the mushrooms into ½-inch slices.

In a large skillet, heat the oil over medium heat. Add the garlic and sauté for about 1 minute. Add the dried mushrooms and sauté, shaking the skillet often, until they start to brown, about 7 minutes. Add the white mushrooms and sauté for 1 minute. Lower the heat, cover the skillet, and cook until the white mushrooms begin to give up their liquid, about 7 minutes. Uncover the skillet and add the red wine, nutmeg, red pepper flakes and the black pepper to taste. Cook for 1 minute longer. Add the basil or parsley and the pine nuts, and toss well. Serve warm.

Grilled Onions

SERVES 4 TO 6

SODIUM PER SERVING: 17 MG
CALORIES PER SERVING: 256

Onions are a particularly good vegetable for grilling. They should be slightly charred on the outside and tender on the inside. Allow one onion per person.

6 medium-sized onions

½ cup olive oil or Basic Marinade (see page 22)
  or Vinaigrette (see page 20)

Peel the onions and pierce them deeply all over with a cooking fork. Roll the onions in the olive oil, marinade, or vinaigrette until coated.

Cook the onions over the grill or hot coals, turning often, until tender, about 30 minutes. Serve right from the grill.

Stuffed Onions

SERVES 4

SODIUM PER SERVING: 17 MG
CALORIES PER SERVING: 161

An onion lover's delight. Grain-based stuffings are good fillings for such other vegetable "containers" as green peppers, eggplants, zucchini and tomatoes. Partially cook the containers — except for tomatoes — before stuffing and baking them.

4 medium-sized sweet onions
1 cup cooked rice
4 tablespoons chopped Apple Ginger Chutney (see page 32)
2 teaspoons unsalted butter

Peel the onions and trim each one so it will stand upright. Put the onions into a large saucepan. Add boiling water to cover. Cook over high heat, covered, until the onions are tender, about 10 minutes. Drain well and set aside to cool.

When the onions are cool enough to handle, use a grapefruit knife to remove the center portion of each one. Chop the centers and reserve 4 tablespoons for the stuffing.

Preheat the oven to 350ºF.

In a bowl, combine the rice, chutney and reserved chopped onion. Mix well and fill each onion shell with the mixture.

Put the stuffed onions into a metal baking dish and add ¼ cup of water. Cover the pan with aluminum foil and bake for 45 minutes. Remove the foil, dot each onion with ½ teaspoon of butter, and place under the broiler until lightly browned, about 5 minutes.

Stir-Fried Parsnips and Carrots

SERVES 4

SODIUM PER SERVING: 54 MG
CALORIES PER SERVING: 200

A splash of good vinegar enhances the flavor of many vegetable dishes. Try different kinds of vinegar for variety — but always use the best quality possible.

2 tablespoons safflower oil
4 parsnips, peeled and cut into ½-inch rounds
4 carrots, peeled and cut into ½-inch rounds
freshly ground black pepper
4 tablespoons chopped fresh parsley
2 tablespoons chopped shallots
1 teaspoon balsamic
   or herb vinegar or more to taste

Heat the safflower oil over high heat in a wok or large skillet. When the oil is very hot, add the parsnips and carrots and sauté, stirring constantly, until golden brown, about 10 minutes. Lower the heat and cook, stirring frequently, until the vegetables are tender but still crisp, about 5 minutes longer. Add black pepper to taste. Add the shallots and cook until softened, about 2 to 3 minutes. Mix in the chopped parsley and sprinkle with the vinegar. Serve immediately.

Baked Potato Fans

SERVES 4

SODIUM PER SERVING: 4 MG
CALORIES PER SERVING: 146

An interesting variation for an old favorite, baked potato fans are attractive to look at and also cook quickly.

2 tablespoons sweet butter, softened
1 teaspoon chopped chives
⅛ teaspoon minced garlic
¼ teaspoon lemon juice
2 large Idaho potatoes

Preheat the oven to 400°F.

Blend together the butter, chives, garlic, and lemon juice in a small bowl. Set aside.

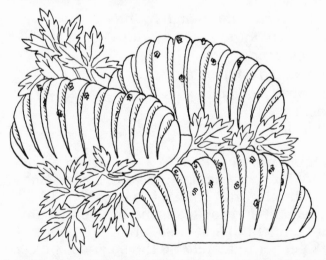

Peel the potatoes and halve them lengthwise. With the cut side down, carefully cut vertical ¼-inch slices through about seven-eighths of each potato half. Be sure not to cut all the way through the bottom of the potato.

Spread 1 teaspoon of the butter mixture over the top of each potato half. Put the potatoes into a greased baking dish and bake until golden brown, about 35 minutes.

Spicy Sautéed Potatoes

SERVES 6

SODIUM PER SERVING: 10 MG
CALORIES PER SERVING: 239

This recipe, as adapted by Sue Dapkins, is Indian in origin. It makes a good buffet dish — so good, in fact, that people tend to eat a lot of it. Be prepared to double the recipe.

2 pounds new potatoes, peeled
⅓ cup safflower oil
2 teaspoons cumin seeds
¼ teaspoon hot red pepper flakes
¼ teaspoon turmeric
1 large onion, diced
1 tablespoon chopped fresh mint
   or ¼ teaspoon dried
1 tablespoon lemon juice
lemon or lime wedges

Cook the potatoes in boiling water to cover until they are just tender. Drain. When cool enough to handle, slice into ¼-inch rounds.

Heat the oil over medium heat in a heavy skillet. Add the cumin seeds and sauté for about 2 minutes, stirring frequently. Add the hot red pepper flakes and the turmeric. Stir again. Add the onion and cook, stirring frequently, until the onions turn an amber color, about 5 minutes. Add the potatoes and toss well. Add the mint and toss again.

Remove the skillet from the heat and sprinkle the potatoes with the lemon juice. Serve garnished with lemon or lime wedges.

Patty Pan Squash with Minted Peas

SERVES 4

SODIUM PER SERVING: 3 MG
CALORIES PER SERVING: 81

Patty pan squash is a pale white member of the summer squash family. It has a saucer-like shape with a scalloped edge. By itself, patty pan squash is delicate in flavor; scooped out, it is a perfect container for other vegetables.

4 medium-sized patty pan squash
1 cup fresh green peas
freshly ground black pepper
1 tablespoon chopped fresh mint
  or 1 teaspoon dried
1 tablespoon unsalted butter

Preheat the oven to 350°F.

Put the squash into a large saucepan filled with 2 inches of water. Cover and simmer gently over medium heat until the squash are tender, about 15 minutes. Remove the squash from the saucepan and set aside to cool.

In a small saucepan, cook the peas in ¼ cup water until just tender, about 5 to 7 minutes. Drain well.

With a teaspoon or grapefruit knife, scoop out and discard the centers of the squash. Remove all the seeds. Put equal amounts of the peas into the center of each squash. Top the peas with black pepper to taste, mint, and butter.

Put the squash into a shallow baking dish filled with 1 inch of water. Cover the dish with aluminum foil and bake until the squash and peas are heated through, about 15 minutes. Serve immediately.

Watercress and Oriental Mushrooms

SERVES 4 TO 6

SODIUM PER SERVING: 95 MG
CALORIES PER SERVING: 91

If fresh watercress is unavailable, substitute 1½ pounds of fresh spinach. Six large, fresh white or woodland mushrooms can be substituted for the dried mushrooms.

2 bunches watercress
8 dried Oriental mushrooms
1 tablespoon vegetable oil
1 tablespoon sesame oil
½ teaspoon chopped ginger

Soak the dried mushrooms in a bowl of warm water until soft, about 20 minutes. Remove the tough stems and slice the mushrooms thinly. Set aside.

Trim away the tough stems of the watercress, then wash the leaves and drain well.

Heat the vegetable and sesame oil in a wok or a large skillet until the oil is very hot. Add the ginger and sauté, stirring constantly, for 1 minute. Add the mushrooms and sauté, stirring constantly, for 2 minutes. Add the watercress and sauté, stirring constantly, until wilted, about 2 minutes longer. Serve immediately.

Yam, Turnip, and Apple Purée

SERVES 4

SODIUM PER SERVING: 57 MG
CALORIES PER SERVING: 474

The apples add natural sweetness to this purée, which goes well with meat and poultry dishes.

4 large yams or sweet potatoes, peeled and quartered
2 medium-sized turnips, peeled and quartered
2 tart apples, peeled, cored and quartered
4 tablespoons unsalted butter, softened
2 tablespoons Apple Ginger Chutney (see page 32)

Put the yams, turnips, and one apple into a saucepan filled with 1 inch of water. Cover the saucepan and cook over medium heat until the yams, turnips, and apple are soft. Drain well.

Put the steamed yams, turnips, and apple into the container of a blender or food processor. Add the butter, the remaining apple and the chutney and process until smooth. To make by hand, chop the uncooked apple and chutney finely with a heavy knife. Combine with the steamed yams, turnips, and apple and the butter. Push the ingredients through a food mill or sieve.

Spoon the purée into a saucepan and cook over low heat, stirring occasionally, until it is warmed through.

Stuffed Zucchini

SERVES 4

SODIUM PER SERVING: 8 MG
CALORIES PER SERVING: 89

As every gardener knows, a new recipe for the prolific zucchini is always welcome. For an interesting variation on this recipe, top each zucchini half with a spoonful of tomato sauce before baking.

4 dried Oriental mushrooms
2 medium-sized zucchini
2 tablespoons olive oil
¼ cup diced carrot
¼ cup diced fennel or celery
¼ cup chopped onion
3 tablespoons chopped parsley
2 garlic cloves, chopped
¼ teaspoon dried thyme
⅛ teaspoon nutmeg
⅛ teaspoon cayenne pepper
⅛ teaspoon wine vinegar
freshly ground black pepper

Put the dried mushrooms into a small bowl and add enough warm water to cover. Soak the mushrooms until they are softened, about 20 minutes. Strain off the soaking liquid, reserving 1 tablespoon. Cut away and discard the tough stems of the mushrooms and chop the caps.

Trim the ends from the zucchini. Put the zucchini into a large pot of boiling water and cook, covered, for 5 minutes. Drain well.

When the zucchini are cool enough to handle, halve them lengthwise. With a spoon, carefully scoop out the flesh and seeds. Chop coarsely and reserve. Reserve the zucchini shells.

Preheat the oven to 375°F.

Heat the olive oil in a skillet. Add the dried mushrooms, carrots, onion, fennel or celery, mushrooms, parsley, garlic, thyme, nutmeg and cayenne pepper. Sauté over medium heat, stirring frequently, for 5 minutes. Add the reserved zucchini and sauté for 2 minutes. Add the vinegar and reserved mushroom soaking liquid and sauté for 2 minutes longer. Season to taste with black pepper and remove the skillet from the heat.

Spoon the vegetable mixture into the reserved zucchini shells. Put the shells into a baking dish and add enough water to fill the dish to a depth of ¼ inch. Bake until lightly browned on top, about 15 to 20 minutes. Serve hot.

Grilled Vegetable Packets

SERVES 4

SODIUM PER SERVING: 6 MG
CALORIES PER SERVING: 56

Any fresh seasonal vegetables can be prepared this way. Cut the vegetables to approximately the same size so that they will cook uniformly. A dot of sweet butter and a few grinds of the peppermill may be substituted for the vinaigrette.

*1 medium-sized zucchini, halved lengthwise and cut
    into 2-inch pieces*
1 medium-sized onion, quartered and thickly sliced
8 cherry tomatoes
*2 tablespoons chopped fresh parsley, basil or thyme
    or 1 teaspoon dried*
4 teaspoons Vinaigrette (see page 20)

Preheat the oven to 400°F. or cook over white coals.

Put equal amounts of zucchini and onion and two cherry tomatoes into the centers of four 6-inch-square pieces of aluminum foil. Top the vegetables with equal amounts of the herbs and sprinkle with the vinaigrette. Fold the foil tightly to make leakproof packets.

Put the packets into the oven or over the coals and cook until tender, about 12 minutes. The vegetables will steam in their own juice. Open the packets and serve with the juices spooned over the vegetables.

Oven-Roasted Vegetables

SERVES 4 TO 6

SODIUM PER SERVING: 49 MG
CALORIES PER SERVING: 244

Oven-roasted vegetables go well with roasted fish, fowl or beef. Small whole vegetables such as unpeeled potatoes, halved baby eggplants, baby beets, and small turnips can be added to or substituted for the vegetables suggested below.

1 fennel bulb, trimmed
4 carrots, peeled
2 onions, halved
4 parsnips, peeled
¾ cup chopped parsley
⅓ cup vegetable oil
freshly ground black pepper

Preheat the oven to 375°F.

Remove the tops and coarse outer stalks from the fennel and quarter the bulb. Put the fennel, carrots, onions and parsnips into a baking dish. Sprinkle with ½ cup of parsley. Pour the oil evenly over the vegetables.

Bake until the vegetables are soft and slightly charred on the outside, about 1 hour. Shake the baking dish frequently as the vegetables cook so that they will cook equally on all sides. Before serving, sprinkle with the remaining parsley and black pepper to taste.

Marinated Vegetables

SERVES 6

SODIUM PER SERVING: 16 MG
CALORIES PER SERVING: 257

Any combination of vegetables, or even only one, will work well
in this recipe. Just be sure the total amount of vegetables used is
about 4 cups. Some suggestions are: green beans, broccoli flowerettes, strips of red and green peppers, whole baby carrots, cauliflower
flowerettes, zucchini spears, celery hearts, and fennel hearts.
This dish is particularly good with cold roast meat or poultry.

4 cups fresh vegetables, cut into bite-sized pieces
⅔ cup olive oil
⅓ cup white wine
¼ cup wine vinegar
½ cup chopped onion
3 garlic cloves, minced
¼ teaspoon dried whole-leaf thyme
⅛ teaspoon cayenne pepper
freshly ground black pepper
1 cup finely chopped parsley

Combine all the ingredients except for ½ cup of the
parsley in a large, heavy pot. Add enough water so that the
vegetables are covered, if necessary. Cover the pot tightly
and cook over medium heat until the vegetables are tender
but still crisp, about 10 minutes.

Remove the pot from the heat. Remove the cover and let
the vegetables cool in the pot. When the vegetables have
cooled, transfer the mixture to a serving dish. Cover the
dish and chill. Serve at room temperature, topped with the
remaining parsley.

Ratatouille

SERVES 4 TO 6
_____
SODIUM PER SERVING: 10 MG
CALORIES PER SERVING: 183

Ratatouille is a dish that originates in the south of France.
It is best made at the end of the summer, when fresh, ripe
tomatoes are in abundance. In addition to the eggplant and zucchini,
try using sweet red or green peppers and other seasonal vegetables.
Ratatouille freezes well and retains its flavor when reheated.
Garnish reheated ratatouille with fresh herbs.

6 medium-sized ripe tomatoes
¼ cup olive oil
1 medium-sized onion, sliced
2 garlic cloves, slivered
1 tablespoon coarsely chopped parsley
1 small eggplant, cut into 1-inch rounds
2 medium-sized zucchini, cut into ¼-inch rounds
3 tablespoons wine vinegar
freshly ground black pepper
2 tablespoons finely chopped fresh parsley
  or fresh basil or fresh oregano

Blanch the tomatoes by placing them in a large pot of
boiling water for about 10 seconds. Drain the tomatoes.
When they are cool enough to handle, peel with a small sharp
knife. Seed and chop the tomatoes, reserving the juice.

Heat the oil in a deep saucepan. Add the onion, garlic
and parsley. Sauté until the onion is soft, about 3 minutes.
Add the eggplant and zucchini and mix well. Cover the
saucepan and simmer over low heat until the vegetables
are tender, about 35 minutes. Add the tomatoes, stir well,
and simmer for 10 minutes longer. Remove the saucepan
from the heat and let stand, covered, for 10 minutes.
Add the wine vinegar and black pepper to taste. Stir well.

Put the ratatouille into a serving dish and garnish with
finely chopped parsley, basil or oregano. Serve warm or
at room temperature.

Desserts

Most of the recipes in this chapter are for fruit-based desserts. We try to preserve the fresh flavor of the fruit by cooking it as little as possible and adding very little sugar. Remember that simple fresh fruit at its seasonal peak is always delicious. Try ripe berries with a sprinkling of rum or eau-de-vie and a dusting of superfine sugar. Another good combination is fresh pineapple chunks with a dash of kirsch. Lemon or lime juice sprinkled over a slice of ripe melon, garnished with a leaf of fresh mint, is a happy ending to a good meal without adding a lot of extra calories.

The natural sugar content of ripe fruit satisfies most sweet tooths. For those who like the crunch of a cookie or prefer a light pastry for that final note of satisfaction, we have included those recipes, too. A complaint often heard about salt-free cooking is that cakes and pastry taste flat and uninteresting. We think such desserts as Orange Walnut Torte and Strawberry Tart with Almond Pastry refute that complaint and prove just how good salt-free baking can be.

Baked Pears in Red Wine

SERVES 6

SODIUM PER SERVING: 6 MG
CALORIES PER SERVING: 167

Good pears are available throughout the fall and winter. For this recipe, use pears that feel a bit firm to the touch. They will emerge from the oven juicy and sweet.

6 ripe, firm pears
3 tablespoons honey
1 teaspoon finely grated ginger
1 cup red wine

Carefully peel the pears, leaving the stems attached. Place them, stem-side up, in a baking dish just large enough to hold the pears upright.

In a small bowl, combine the honey and ginger. Drizzle the mixture over the pears. Pour half the wine over the pears. Cover the dish with aluminum foil and bake, basting often with the remaining wine, until the pears are soft, about 45 minutes.

Remove the foil and let the pears cool in the pan. Serve with pan juices spooned over each pear.

Baked Pears with Walnuts

SERVES 4

SODIUM PER SERVING: 4 MG
CALORIES PER SERVING: 221

This dessert can be prepared in advance and baked while the main course is being served. Any nut may be substituted for the walnuts; substitute apple or orange juice for the rum.

4 firm, ripe pears, halved and cored
juice of ½ lemon
4 teaspoons dark rum (optional)
½ cup chopped walnuts
2 teaspoons honey

Preheat the oven to 350°F.

Put the pears into a baking dish and sprinkle them with the lemon juice and rum.

Sprinkle the chopped nuts over the pears.
Drizzle some honey over each pear.

Add enough water to the baking dish to fill it to a depth of ¼ inch. Cover the dish with aluminum foil.

Bake until the pears are just tender, about 20 to 25 minutes. Serve warm.

Apples Baked with Cider

SERVES 4

SODIUM PER SERVING: LESS THAN 0.5 MG
CALORIES PER SERVING: 192

The apple flavor of this dessert is given a boost by the Calvados, which is French apple brandy, or applejack. Red wine or regular brandy may be used instead. Serve it with vanilla ice cream.

6 medium-sized apples, peeled, cored and thinly sliced
3 tablespoons lemon juice
2 tablespoons Calvados
2 tablespoons unsalted butter
apple cider

Preheat the oven to 375ºF.

Arrange the apple slices in a glass or ceramic baking dish. Sprinkle with the lemon juice and Calvados and dot with the butter. Add enough apple cider to fill the dish to a depth of 1 inch.

Bake for 20 minutes. Serve warm or chilled.

Fresh Fruit Whip

SERVES 4

SODIUM PER SERVING: 91 MG
CALORIES PER SERVING: 221

This refreshing dessert can be made with almost any ripe fruit or berry. Bananas, peaches, plums, nectarines, blueberries — all are good. It will keep well in the freezer for up to a week. The simplest garnish is sliced fresh fruit. For more variety, try chopped nuts, thin lemon slices, mint leaves or a sprinkling of fruit brandy or light rum. If the egg whites are omitted, this becomes a good recipe for frozen yogurt.

1½ cups mashed ripe fruit or berries
1 cup unflavored low-fat yogurt
½ cup sugar
½ teaspoon cinnamon
4 egg whites

If such fruit as peaches or plums is being used, peel the fruit, remove the stems and pits, and mash. If berries are being used, wash well and hull, then mash. Put the mashed fruit into a mixing bowl. Add the yogurt, sugar, and cinnamon and mix well.

In another bowl, beat the egg whites until stiff. Fold the egg whites into the fruit mixture.

To serve immediately, spoon the fruit whip into parfait or wine glasses or dessert bowls. Garnish with fresh fruit. To serve later, cover the bowl with plastic wrap and freeze. Remove the bowl from the freezer, thaw the fruit whip for 5 to 10 minutes, then spoon it into serving glasses or bowls and garnish.

Fresh Fruit Salad

SERVES 4

SODIUM PER SERVING: 22 MG
CALORIES PER SERVING: 97

Fruit salad is most fun to eat when everyone selects pieces from one platter and dips them into a communal bowl of sauce. However, you could put the fruit into dessert bowls and top with the sauce instead.

4 cups fresh, ripe seasonal fruit, cut into bite-sized pieces
½ cup unflavored low-fat yogurt
3 tablespoons Apple Ginger Chutney (see page 32)
1 tablespoon orange juice

Arrange the fruit around the outside of a large serving platter.

In a small bowl, combine the yogurt, chutney, and orange juice. Mix until smooth. Put the sauce into a small serving bowl and place the bowl in the center of the serving platter. Serve with small forks for dipping.

Sliced Mangos with Raspberry Sauce

SERVES 4

SODIUM PER SERVING: 8 MG
CALORIES PER SERVING: 136

This raspberry sauce is also delicious over papayas, peaches, and pears. Purée the raspberries quickly so the seeds don't become bitter.

1 pint fresh raspberries or 1 10-ounce package
  thawed frozen raspberries
2 to 3 tablespoons sugar (optional)
juice of 1 lemon
2 large, ripe mangos

Quickly purée the raspberries in a food processor or blender. Add the sugar and lemon juice, stir well, and set aside.

Peel the mangos and cut them into thin slices.

Spoon the raspberry sauce onto individual serving plates. Arrange slices of mango on top of the sauce and serve.

Brandied Fruit

MAKES 1 CROCK

SODIUM PER SERVING (3 OUNCES): 1 MG
CALORIES PER SERVING: 72

With a fruit crock in the pantry, dessert is always ready.
Any large, decorative jar with a tightly fitting lid will do.
Use such fruit as peaches, plums, apricots, varieties of grapes,
cherries, and various berries. Select only unblemished, perfectly
ripe fruit. Serve the brandied fruit alone in a stemmed glass with
sprigs of mint, or use the fruit as a topping for ice cream,
sherbets, or plain cake.

assortment of seasonal ripe whole fruits
brandy or dark rum

Remove the stems from the fruit; leave the fruit whole.
Peel larger fruits such as peaches and plums. Carefully
place the fruits into a clean, large crock or glass jar with
a tightly fitting lid. Fill the crock completely, but do not
crowd the fruit.

Add enough brandy or dark rum to completely cover the
fruit. Cover the crock tightly and store at room temperature.
Let stand for 3 to 4 weeks before using. Additional fruit
may be added to the mixture as the original fruit is used.
Mix well after each addition and add enough brandy
or rum to cover the added fruit.

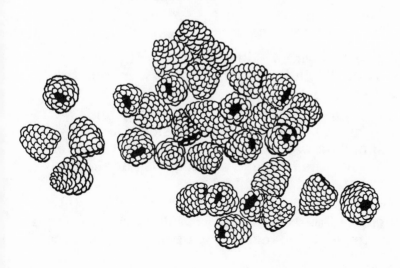

Susan's Bourbon Peaches

MAKES 3 PINTS

SODIUM PER SERVING (1 CUP): 4 MG
CALORIES PER SERVING: 674

Serve these peaches with Lemon Ginger Thins (see page 181)
or with vanilla yogurt.

4 pounds ripe, unblemished peaches
7 cups water
3½ cups sugar
rind of 1 large lemon, cut into 3 pieces
1½ cups Bourbon whiskey

Put the water and sugar into a large saucepan. Bring to
boil over high heat, stirring frequently. When the sugar
has dissolved, add the lemon rind and boil for 1 minute.
Reduce the heat and add the peaches. Simmer the peaches
in the syrup for 15 minutes, turning them occasionally.

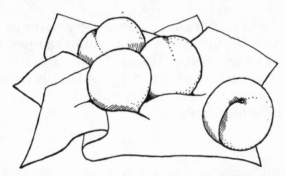

Remove the peaches with a slotted spoon; continue
to cook the syrup. When the peaches are cool enough to
handle, peel them.

Sterilize 3 1-pint jars by washing them with soap and
very hot water and then placing them, upside-down, in 4
to 5 inches of boiling water. Boil the jars over low heat for
8 minutes. Turn off the heat and add the lids and rings to
the hot water. Let stand for 3 minutes.

Divide the peaches among the jars while the jars are still
hot. Add ½ cup of Bourbon to each jar. Fill the jars to within
½ inch of the top with the reduced syrup, making sure the

peaches are completely covered. Run a knife down along the insides of the jars to release any air bubbles. Top each jar with a piece of the lemon rind. Seal the jars tightly with the hot lids. Cool the jars in a draft-free area overnight. The next day, check the seals by turning the jars upside-down or pressing the center of the inner lids. If there is no leakage or if the inner lids do not move, then the jars are sealed properly.

Store the peaches in a cool, dark place for 1 month before serving.

Whole Wheat Bread Pudding

SERVES 6

SODIUM PER SERVING: 202 MG
CALORIES PER SERVING: 214

Basic bread pudding is among the simplest of desserts — and a great starting point for your cooking creativity. Try topping this pudding with fresh berries before baking, or adding raisins or grated orange rind to the liquid ingredients before cooking. Serve it topped with Lemon Sauce or Blueberry Spice Sauce (see page 176).

4 cups whole wheat bread cubes, crusts removed
3 eggs, lightly beaten
2¾ cups low-fat milk
2 teaspoons cinnamon
½ cup firmly packed brown sugar

Preheat the oven to 375°F.

Grease a medium-sized baking dish.

Spread the bread cubes in the baking dish.

In a large bowl, combine the eggs, milk, cinnamon, and brown sugar. Mix well and pour over the bread cubes. Let stand until the bread cubes have absorbed the mixture, about 10 to 15 minutes.

Bake until a knife inserted into the center of the pudding comes out clean, about 40 minutes.

Serve warm, topped with a fruit sauce.

Lemon Sauce

MAKES 3½ CUPS

SODIUM PER SERVING (¼ CUP): LESS THAN 0.5 MG
CALORIES PER SERVING: 90

Lemon sauce is delicious as a topping for bread pudding, plain cakes, fresh fruit desserts and ices, and especially meringue cake.

1 cup sugar
2 tablespoons cornstarch
2 cups cold water
¼ cup unsalted butter
¼ cup lemon juice
3 tablespoons grated lemon zest

In a saucepan over low heat, combine the sugar and cornstarch. Slowly add the cold water and mix well. Bring the mixture to a boil and add the butter, lemon juice, and grated lemon rind. Continue to boil slowly until the sauce becomes thick and opaque, about 10 minutes.

Blueberry Spice Sauce

MAKES 3 CUPS

SODIUM PER SERVING (¼ CUP): LESS THAN 0.5 MG
CALORIES PER SERVING: 32

Try this sauce on French toast or pancakes. Omit the sugar for a sauce that is tarter and lower in calories.

¼ cup sugar (optional)
1 cup water
1 teaspoon cinnamon
¼ teaspoon nutmeg
2 tablespoons lemon juice
2 cups fresh blueberries

Combine the sugar, water, cinnamon, nutmeg, and lemon juice in a saucepan over low heat. Stir until the sugar is dissolved and slowly bring to a boil. Simmer for 5 minutes. Add the blueberries and simmer for 2 minutes more. Remove from the heat.

Peach Ice

SERVES 4 TO 6
_____

SODIUM PER SERVING: 2 MG
CALORIES PER SERVING: 169

No special equipment is needed to make this dessert. Although the
recipe calls for ripe peaches, any fresh fruit or berry or melon purée
will make a delicious ice. The amount of sugar added to the purée
will vary according to the ripeness of the fruit. As a general rule, add
about ¼ cup sugar to each cup of purée.

2 pounds ripe peaches
½ cup water
¾ cup sugar
2 tablespoons lemon juice

Peel the peaches by immersing them for 3 minutes in
boiling water. When the peaches are cool enough to handle,
slip off the skins. Halve the peaches and remove the pits.
Cut the halves into large pieces and purée them in a food
processor or blender. There should be about 3 cups of purée.

In a small saucepan combine the sugar and water. Bring to
a boil over medium heat, stirring frequently. Reduce the heat
and simmer, stirring frequently, for 5 minutes. Remove the
saucepan from the heat and let the syrup cool.

Put the peach purée, syrup, and lemon juice into a large
mixing bowl. Add additional sugar or lemon juice to taste.
Mix well.

Pour the mixture into a shallow metal baking dish or into
several metal ice-cube trays from which the partitions have
been removed. Put the dish or trays into the freezer. Freeze
until the mixture is firm, about 3 hours. Stir the mixture
every hour to break up the ice particles.

Remove the ice from the freezer 10 minutes before
serving. Spoon the ice into individual serving bowls or
stemmed glasses. Garnish each serving with peach slices,
mint sprigs, or a spoonful of berries.

Strawberry Tart with Almond Pastry

MAKES 1 9-INCH TART; SERVES 8

SODIUM PER SERVING: 7 MG
CALORIES PER SERVING: 278

Use fresh raspberries or blueberries instead of or in addition
to the strawberries in this recipe. If you wish, sprinkle 2 tablespoons
of toasted, slivered or sliced almonds over the glazed berries.
The same dough that makes the tart shell here can be rolled out,
cut into shapes, sprinkled with sugar and cinnamon, and baked
at 375°F. until slightly browned for delicious cookies.

¾ cup flour
⅓ cup ground toasted almonds
3 tablespoons sugar
6 tablespoons unsalted butter
1 egg yolk, lightly beaten
¾ cup red currant or strawberry jelly
2 pints hulled fresh strawberries

Preheat the oven to 400°F.

In a mixing bowl combine the flour, almonds, and sugar. Using a pastry blender or two knives, or in a food processor, cut in the butter by tablespoons until the mixture resembles coarse crumbs. Add the egg yolk and mix until the crumbs form a dough.

Roll out the dough ¼-inch thick on a lightly floured surface. Fit the dough into a 9-inch tart pan with a removable bottom. Line the dough with a sheet of aluminum foil and weight down the foil with a handful of dried beans or rice. Bake for 10 minutes. Lower the oven temperature to 350°F., remove the foil and dried beans or rice, and continue baking until the pastry is golden, about 5 minutes longer. Remove from the oven and let cool. Remove the tart shell from the pan. Cool the tart shell completely on a wire rack.

In a small saucepan, heat the jelly with 2 teaspoons of water. When the jelly is completely melted, let it cool slightly and then brush half of it carefully over the inside of the tart shell. Let cool.

Arrange the strawberries, pointed-end up, in the tart shell. Glaze the strawberries with the remaining jelly, reheating it if necessary. Let the glaze cool before serving.

Mango Sorbet

SERVES 4 TO 6

SODIUM PER SERVING: 19 MG
CALORIES PER SERVING: 138

A sorbet is an ice that has egg white added to it.
This recipe can also be made with ripe papayas.

3 large, ripe mangos
¼ cup water
⅓ cup sugar
3 tablespoons lime juice
1 egg white, lightly beaten

Peel the mangos and remove the large pits.
Cut the mangos into large chunks and purée them in a
food processor or blender.

In a small saucepan combine the water and the sugar.
Bring the mixture to a boil over medium heat, stirring
frequently. Reduce the heat and simmer, stirring frequently,
for 5 minutes. Remove the saucepan from the heat and
let the syrup cool.

Put the mango purée, syrup, and lime juice into a large
mixing bowl. Add additional sugar or lime juice to taste.
Mix well.

Pour the mixture into a shallow metal baking dish.
Put the dish into the freezer until the mixture just begins to
get firm. Remove the dish from the freezer and fold in the egg
white. Return the dish to the freezer until the sorbet is
firm, about 3 hours. Stir the sorbet every hour to break
up the ice particles.

Remove the sorbet from the freezer 10 minutes
before serving. Spoon it into individual serving bowls
or stemmed glasses. Garnish each serving with mango
slices, mint sprigs, or a spoonful of berries.

Lemon Ginger Thins

MAKES 3 DOZENS COOKIES

SODIUM PER SERVING (4 COOKIES): 2 MG
CALORIES PER SERVING: 173

Serve these elegant, crunchy cookies by themselves,
with an ice or sorbet, or with fruit salad.

1 cup flour
1 teaspoon powdered ginger
¼ teaspoon nutmeg
¼ teaspoon cinnamon
¼ teaspoon ground cloves
4 tablespoons unsalted butter, softened
3 tablespoons brown sugar
3 tablespoons sugar
½ teaspoon grated lemon rind
1 teaspoon dark rum
1 teaspoon lemon extract

Sift together the flour, ginger, nutmeg, cinnamon and cloves.

Using an electric mixer, cream the butter in a medium-sized
bowl. Gradually add the brown sugar and the sugar, beating
well after addition. Add the lemon rind, rum, and lemon
extract and beat well. Add the flour and spices mixture and
beat well. Cover the bowl with plastic wrap and refrigerate
for 4 hours.

Preheat the oven to 350°F. Line several baking sheets
with aluminum foil.

Remove the dough from the refrigerator.
Cut off ¼ of the dough and return the rest to the
refrigerator. Using a floured rolling pin, roll the dough out
on a floured surface to ⅛-inch thick. Cut out cookies from
the dough, using a cookie cutter or glass about 3 inches
in diameter. Repeat with the remaining dough.

Put the cookies close together on a baking sheet. Bake until
golden, about 8 minutes. Put the cookies on racks to cool.
When thoroughly cooled, store in an airtight container.

Oatmeal Banana Chocolate Chip Bars

MAKES 24 BARS

SODIUM PER SERVING (1 BAR): 10 MG
CALORIES PER SERVING: 164

These bars freeze well. In fact, they are particularly delicious when served partially thawed.

1 cup firmly packed brown sugar
½ cup unsalted butter
2 eggs, slightly beaten
1 teaspoon vanilla extract
⅛ teaspoon cinnamon
2 cups rolled oats
2 cups unbleached flour
2 ripe bananas, mashed
½ cup chocolate chips

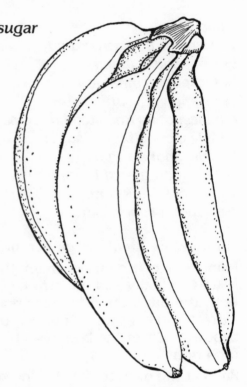

Preheat the oven to 350°F. Grease and flour an 8 x 8-inch square baking pan.

Cream together the brown sugar and the butter.
Mix until fluffy. Add the eggs, vanilla, and cinnamon.
Continue mixing until all ingredients are well blended.
Add the oats and flour and blend briefly. Stir in the mashed bananas and the chocolate chips.

Pour the batter into the baking pan. Bake until a toothpick inserted into the center comes out clean, about 35 minutes.

When done, remove the baking pan from the oven and cool on a rack for 15 minutes. Cut into rectangles.

Orange Walnut Torte

MAKES 1 9-INCH CAKE; SERVES 8

SODIUM PER SERVING: 20 MG
CALORIES PER SERVING: 393

This elegant torte is quite easy to make. Two ounces of grated unsweetened chocolate may be added to the batter for extra richness. Serve with Lemon Sauce (see page 176) poured over the torte.

1¾ *cups unbleached flour*
1 *cup sugar*
3 *teaspoons low-sodium baking powder*
½ *teaspoon cinnamon*
¼ *teaspoon ground cloves*
¼ *teaspoon nutmeg*
¼ *teaspoon allspice*
⅓ *cup vegetable oil*
⅔ *cup low-fat milk*
1 *teaspoon vanilla extract*
1 *egg, lightly beaten*
1 *cup chopped walnuts*
grated rind of 1 orange
2 *tablespoons orange juice*

Preheat the oven to 350°F. Lightly grease and flour a 9x9-inch square baking pan.

In a mixing bowl sift together the flour, sugar, baking powder, cinnamon, cloves, nutmeg, and allspice. Stir in the oil, milk, vanilla and egg. Add the walnuts, orange rind, and orange juice. Mix thoroughly and pour into the baking pan.

Bake until a toothpick inserted into the center of the torte comes out clean, about 30 to 35 minutes. Remove the pan from the oven and cool on a rack for 30 minutes.

To serve, turn the torte out onto a platter and slice. Top with a fruit sauce.

Meringue Cake

MAKES 1 CAKE; SERVES 8

SODIUM PER SERVING: 50 MG
CALORIES PER SERVING: 89

Meringue cake is a perfect base for a topping of fresh fruit or berries, grated chocolate or slivered almonds. Serve this cake topped with Lemon Sauce or Blueberry Spice Sauce (see page 176).

8 egg whites
1 teaspoon lemon juice
¾ cup sugar
½ teaspoon almond extract

Preheat the oven to 350ºF. Heavily grease a bundt pan with vegetable oil.

In a mixing bowl begin beating the egg whites, by hand or with an electric mixer. As they just begin to get firm, add the sugar by teaspoons, beating well after each addition. Add the almond extract. Continue beating until the mixture holds its shape.

Carefully spoon the meringue into the bundt pan, making sure there are no air pockets. Cover the top of the meringue with waxed paper and put the bundt pan into a larger round pan. Add enough water to the larger pan to come halfway up the sides of the bundt pan. Bake until the meringue is firm and dry, about 30 to 35 minutes. Remove the pan from the oven and put it on a cooling rack. Cool the meringue completely in the pan before turning it out onto a serving platter.

Entertaining

The menus in this chapter are designed to help you plan special
meals. Most of the recipes come from chapters of this book.
The others, in most cases, are suggestions for fresh fruits and
vegetables, prepared simply and presented attractively. We have
tried to plan the menus so that most of the preparation can be
done before the guests arrive.

Always use the best and freshest possible seasonal produce.
Since not everything will always be available, use these menus as
outlines subject to change with the season, the market supply, the
guest list, and the preferences of the cook. Substitutions in the
menus can also be easily made to accommodate guests who are
vegetarians or on medically restricted diets.

Sam Aaron, noted author and lecturer on wine and president
of Sherry Lehmann, the world-famous wine dealers in New York City,
has added his expert suggestions for wines to accompany each
menu. Of course, if you prefer, such libations as fruit punch, apple
cider, iced tea, beer, or mineral water will also complement any
of the menus.

Summer Barbecue

bowls of Spiced Nuts (page 36)
Chilled Yogurt Soup (page 57)
Lime-Broiled Fish Steaks with Mustard and Ginger (page 71)
Grilled Onions (page 158)
brochettes of red and yellow cherry tomatoes
Chutney Rice (page 134)
Peach Ice (page 177)
Wine: Muscadet (Chateau de Cleray 1983, Loire, France)

Picnic for Six

Bulgur Wheat Salad (page 127) wrapped in lettuce leaves
Lamb and Roast Pepper Salad (page 96)
Ratatouille (page 168)
Onion Bread (page 137) and assorted crackers
Dilly Beans (page 30)
fresh fruit
Lemon Ginger Thins (page 181)
Wine: Chardonnay (Bald Eagle 1982, Sonoma, California)

Holiday Menu for Twelve

crudites with Basic Yogurt Dressing (page 21)
Turkey Broth (page 108) with vegetables
Holiday Roast Turkey (page 109)
Old-Fashioned Bread Stuffing (page 110)
Sesame Green Beans (page 144)
Yam, Turnip, and Apple Puree (page 163)
Apple Ginger Chutney (page 32)
Megan's Cranberry Velvet Conserve (page 28)
fresh fruit
Orange Walnut Torte (page 183)
Wine: Brut sparkling wine (Boyer, Haut Savoie, France)
served before main course; Brouilly (Chateau de la Chaize
1983, Grand Cru Beaujolais, France) served slightly chilled

Hors d'Oeuvres Buffet for Twenty

cucumber spears with chili powder and lime
Salsa (page 41) with salt-free corn chips
Seviche (page 40)
Eggplant Salad (page 35) with Pita Brittle (page 42)
Grilled Kebabs (page 34)
Spicy Chicken Wings (page 36)
fresh fruit with chutney-yogurt dip
Wine: Rioja (Marques de Caceres 1978, Spain)

Summer Brunch for Six

fresh fruits and berries
Fresh Mozzarella, Tomato, and Basil (page 44)
Pasta Salad with Salmon and Peas (page 126)
Dilled Cucumber Salad (page 42)
thin whole wheat toast triangles
Strawberry Tart with Almond Pastry (page 178)
Wine: Sancerre 1983 (Upper Loire Valley, France) served with
pasta salad; Kir (3 ounces creme de cassis mixed with 1 bottle
dry white wine and served over ice in long-stemmed glasses)
before and after

Summer Dinner Party for Eight

Gazpacho (page 53)
Baked Whole Fish (page 79)
new potatoes with fresh herbs
fresh corn
watercress salad
Sliced Mangos with Raspberry Sauce (page 172)
Wine: Napa Brut sparkling wine (Domaine Chandon, Napa,
California) before dinner; Corvo Bianco 1983 (Sicily, Italy)
with meal

Winter Brunch for Six

Citrus and Onion Salad (page 63)
Fisherman's Soup (page 52)
Herbed Biscuits (page 139)
green salad with endive
Orange Walnut Torte (page 183)
Wine: Blanc de Blancs (La Vieille Ferme 1983, Southeast
Rhone Valley, France)

Winter Dinner Party for Eight

oysters on the half shell
Roast Fillet of Beef with Green Peppercorns (page 87)
Barley Casserole with Dried Mushrooms (page 132)
Stir-Fried Parsnips and Carrots (page 159)
Citrus and Onion Salad (page 63)
Baked Pears with Walnuts (page 170)
Lemon Ginger Thins (page 181)
Wines: Chablis (Louis Michel 1983, France) with oysters;
Bordeaux (Chateau Gloria 1979, St. Julien, France) with beef;
Sandeman Founders Port (Portugal) with pears

Index

About Lifespice

Lifespice is a line of salt-free condiments and dressings that are all natural and free of preservatives. The dressings contain no sweeteners, although the condiments have some honey added for sweetness. Of course, none of the products contain any salt or salt substitutes, ever.

These fine food products have been created for table-top use to add interesting flavors to prepared foods. They are also excellent when used in cooking.

Each Lifespice product contains a custom-ground blend of herbs and spices. Because we use the best quality ingredients, the products are highly concentrated. Just a spoonful or two is all you usually need.

Whenever *The Lifespice Salt-Free Cookbook* calls for condiments such as mustard, chutney, tomato bases, barbecue sauce or vinaigrette, you may substitute the equivalent Lifespice product.

Lifespice products are available in most fine food stores, department stores and specialty supermarkets, as well as by mail.

Please write to us for information. We are always pleased to hear from you and help in any way we can with ideas, suggestions and recipes for salt-free cooking.

Lifespice
60 West 15 Street
New York, N.Y. 10010